Language Through the Looking Glass

Language Through the Looking Glass

Exploring Language and Linguistics

MARINA YAGUELLO

Adapted from the original French by
Trevor Harris and the author

OXFORD UNIVERSITY PRESS

Oxford University Press, Great Clarendon Street, Oxford OX2 6DP

Oxford New York

Athens Auckland Bangkok Bogotá Buenos Aires Calcutta
Cape Town Chennai Dar es Salaam Delhi Florence Hong Kong Istanbul
Karachi Kuala Lumpur Madrid Melbourne Mexico City Mumbai
Nairobi Paris São Paolo Singapore Taipei Tokyo Toronto Warsaw

and associated companies in
Berlin Ibadan

Oxford is a registered trade mark of Oxford University Press

Published in the United States
by Oxford University Press Inc., New York

British Library Cataloguing in Publication Data
Data available

Library of Congress Cataloging in Publication Data
Language through the looking glass: exploring language and
linguistics/Marina Yaguello; adapted from the original French by
Trevor Harris and the author.
Significantly rev. and updated version of the author's
Alice au pays du langage.
1. Language and languages. 2. Linguistics. I. Harris, Trevor A.
Le V. II. Yaguello, Marina. Alice au pays du langage. III. Title.
P106.Y34   1998   400—dc21   98-7376
ISBN 0-19-870005-9 (Pbk)
ISBN 0-19-870006-7 (Hbk)

10 9 8 7 6 5 4 3 2

Typeset by Hope Services (Abingdon) Ltd.
Printed in Great Britain on acid-free paper by
Biddles Ltd., Guildford & King's Lynn

Preface

Why Through a Looking Glass?

Alice and I go back a long way. As a child, mesmerized by the Disney film—the first I had ever seen—I tried to copy her. It was only later that I discovered Carroll's text, at an age when nobody reads fairy tales any more. It was the original English, fortunately, since I might otherwise have missed, among the countless facets of *Alice*, the one that fascinates me most: its language.

The Alice books, for anyone who is interested in linguistics, provide constant food for thought and constant delight. By playing with the English language, it is language in general which Lewis Carroll is calling into question. Over the years, it occurred to me that it was quite possible to write an introduction to linguistics that would be based entirely on wordplay. But this would be linguistics shorn of its austerity. *Alice au pays du langage* was written, accordingly, drawing many examples from the Alice books as well as from poetry and from the lore and language of schoolchildren.

When the opportunity came to prepare an English version of the book, I was, in a sense, faced with the opposite set of difficulties to those which I had encountered in the original French version: there, I had had to limit my references to *Alice*, while freely exploiting a whole range of appropriate French examples. Now that Alice finds herself back among her own kind, I have had to eliminate many of my French examples and hunt down additional material in English which made the same, or a similar point. At the same time I have significantly revised and updated the original book, while retaining its spirit.

Although it provides an introduction to the study of language, this book is not intended to be used solely in an academic setting. It is my hope that its readership may include students and lovers of language alike.

I particularly wish to thank my editor at Oxford University Press, Frances Morphy, for encouraging me to rewrite this book almost entirely, for pointing out errors and obscurities, and for offering no end of useful suggestions. Although she has helped me produce a more readable and better structured book any errors that may remain are my own responsibility.

M.Y.

March 1997

Illustration Sources

The publishers wish to thank the following who have kindly given permission to reproduce illustrations on the pages indicated.

10 © Hergé/Moulinsart 1998; 11 Peter Newark's Military Pictures; 27 Lucky Luke Productions; 49 Reproduced by permission of The Agency (London) Ltd. Copyright © 1997 Graham Rawle. First published by Fourth Estate Limited 1997. All rights reserved and enquiries to The Agency (London) Ltd, 24 Pottery Lane, London W11 4LZ, Fax: 0171 727 9037; 75 © 1998 Les Editions Albert René/Goscinny—Uderzo; 85 Batman and all related elements are trademarks of DC Comics © 1998. All rights reserved. Used with permission; 106 The Far Side by Gary Larson © 1991 Farworks, Inc. Used with permission. All rights reserved.

Contents

Introduction

So, you are a linguist . . .

'So, you are a linguist. . . . Is there a book that you would recommend? . . . I would really like to understand what linguistics is about.' This is a common query addressed to linguists and I usually suggest reading the work of such popular linguists as Émile Benveniste, Dwight Bolinger, Roman Jakobson, or John Lyons, whose writing—and, therefore, whose thinking—is so wonderfully clear, whatever the complexity of the subject they may be dealing with. But for a non-specialist this is not always easy reading, to say nothing of the Chomskian literature or the more recent functional and cognitive linguistics trends, the technical nature of which will only discourage those who are simply curious about language. As for textbooks proper, aimed at a student audience, their format may not appeal to a non-student readership.

This book undertakes, by way of contrast, to teach something to the largest possible audience. I have therefore attempted to make it as unacademic as possible, aiming at readers whom I take to have no prior knowledge of linguistics or of its jargon.

I would argue, nevertheless, that in the pages which follow, you will find everything you need to know if—although not a linguist in the strict sense—you *love language* and are fascinated by it. In addition, to all those people who may have been put off by theoretical linguistics which, all too often, hides its identity as a social (hence imprecise) science beneath mounds of mathematical formulae, I would like to show that beyond that dry-as-dust surface, linguistics can be appealing, fun, and quite, quite accessible. The use of a specific jargon, or metalanguage, can and will be kept to a strict minimum. It cannot, however, be entirely eliminated: it would not be realistic to believe that we can talk about language and linguistics using only everyday language.[1]

Among humankind's cultural tools, language occupies a very special place: human beings are programmed to speak, to learn languages—whichever ones they may be—but not to learn physics, say, or mathematics. Indeed, language responds to a fundamental human need: namely, the

---

[1] All technical terms are listed in the index. Page numbers in bold indicate the places where detailed discussion of the particular term is to be found.

need to communicate, which, unlike the need to eat, breathe, sleep or make love, does not manifest itself in a 'natural' way. Language has to be learnt in the form of a *language system* belonging to a particular *speech community*, in order to be manifested in *speech acts*. While the potential *ability* to speak is genetic, therefore, its realization requires a cultural learning process: a fact confirmed by the many documented cases of unsocialized, 'feral' children—or *enfants sauvages*, to use the established French term—whose capacity for speaking has become atrophied.

Language is also special in another way. It controls a specifically human ability for symbolization and abstraction. Humankind can evoke not only what is present and palpable, but also what is distant (in time or space), abstract, or even imaginary. 'In the beginning was the Word' and there is no human thought without words.[2]

But I am just as interested in speakers as in the nature of language itself. I would like to have the reader discover what I would call a *speaker-oriented* approach to linguistics. For me, the speaker is at the very heart of language. This means that the study of language can never be divorced from references to the speaker, his or her background, character, and experience. It is therefore by starting from our own experience as language-users, that we will best be able to analyse the language phenomenon.

But linguistics has one characteristic which distinguishes it from all other sciences: it can only apprehend its subject matter, describe it and analyse it, by using language itself. We must therefore posit what is known as a *metalinguistic* relationship between language as *subject matter* for analysis and language used as a *tool* for that analysis. From this it follows that while you have to be a sociologist to do sociology and a mathematician to do mathematics, there is a form of intuitive, pre-theoretical, spontaneous linguistics which is practised by *all* speakers merely because they *are* speakers. Language belongs to everyone. Practical experience of language is at the very heart of the activity of all human beings. Linguists do not have a monopoly on linguistics in the way that physicists do on physics. We all do linguistics, even though we clearly need to draw a line between the linguistics of the 'naive' native speaker (sometimes called folk linguistics) and scientific linguistics.

Every speaker is steeped in *metalinguistic activity*. This can be *conscious*, when contrasting, defining, paraphrasing words or utterances or *unconscious*, in the complex process of 'spontaneously' acquiring one's native language.

---

[2] A fascinating testimony of this is given by Helen Keller in her celebrated autobiography. She explains how the world was revealed to her at the age of 7 when she understood the nature of words. This of course does not mean that no form of mental activity is possible outside articulated language (babies, the language impaired, or even animals certainly do 'think'), but it is obvious that our more elaborate thinking processes rely on words.

There is one significant area where all that metalinguistic activity is brought back into full view: wordplay, playing *on* words, playing *with* words, verbal play in all its forms—punning, the rebus, charades, spoonerisms, eye rhymes, nursery rhymes, riddles, portmanteau words, crosswords, anagrams, and so on: everything in our speech which reveals an innate, intuitive linguistics in speakers. Playing, after all, presupposes that one knows the rules and how to bend them, how to exploit the ambiguity which characterizes natural languages, as well as the creativity which they allow. For children, language-learning is inseparable from word games, which thereby take on educational value (mainly self-educational as it turns out). Indeed, all wordplay presupposes correct acquisition of the code. Poor knowledge of the language would mean poor wordplay. The ability to play with words is a measure of language proficiency.

Poetry is another way of playing with words, for play and poetry are united in their *gratuitousness*. Words are to the poet what sound is to the musician or clay to the sculptor: a living substance to be fashioned with love and for pleasure. Swift, Lewis Carroll, Edward Lear, James Joyce, e. e. cummings, T. S. Eliot, Jack Kerouac, Gertrude Stein, Anthony Burgess, William Burroughs, to name only a few, have all been fascinated by language and have tried to expose its structure and explore its limits.

A number of language features which are the object of serious research are highlighted in *Alice's Adventures in Wonderland* and *Through the Looking-Glass*. These two books written about children and for children by an adult who had remained a child, have fascinated adults—especially linguists—for more than a century.

What Lewis Carroll had already sensed (but obviously not explicated as a piece of theory), well before Chomsky, was the non-finite character imparted to language by the rule known as *recursiveness*, which allows the embedding of clauses ad infinitum. Similarly, Carroll reacted in advance against the pre-eminence structuralism was later to give to sounds—i.e. *form*—over meaning. Typically, Carroll expressed his preference in the following subversion of a well-known saying: 'Take care of the *sense* and the *sounds* will take care of themselves.'

Lewis Carroll shows us with great clarity the link between language and play. In many ways, his work represents a profound reflection on the nature of language, in which theoretical implications for modern-day linguists are concealed by the fun. Perhaps what we need to admit is that poets and children—the language-users who know best how to play with language and derive pleasure from it—may ultimately have as much to teach us about language as the specialists. Linguistics, it would seem, is far too serious a business to be left to linguists alone!

Wordplay, based on unconscious metalinguistic activity, reveals the linguistic competence of the speaking subject and we can argue that the *poetic* function, which subsumes the *play* function, is central among the different functions of language: human communication can be distinguished from other forms of communication by the very fact that its purpose is not exclusively to convey information.

It is not my ambition to cover the whole field of linguistics, nor even to mention all of its theories, methods, or aims. In any event, there still exists no single theory or description capable of accounting for the language phenomenon as a whole, for a specific language, or even for part of a language. Linguistics is a diabolically difficult science (if science it really is) where, although so much seems to have already been accomplished, nearly everything still remains to be done. Even the subject matter and ultimate purpose of linguistics are constantly a matter of debate. A number of its concepts remain hazy and controversial. Agreement is yet to be reached, even on such basic points as what constitutes the *sign* (and its arbitrary nature), on what comes under *language system* and what comes under *speech act*, on the relations between syntax, semantics, and pragmatics, even on the notion of meaning; not to mention disagreements about basic descriptive terminology. One French linguist has put the case rather pessimistically:

Linguistics has consisted of vain attempts to define various concepts whose sole common denominator has been their resistance to the act of definition. So much so that Kramsky (1969) wrote that 'linguistics is that science which is at war with its definitions'. Indeed, one only has to consider the abundance and diversity of definitions put forward for the phoneme, the syllable and, more recently, the sentence, to realize that 'we are pessimistic as to the possibility of defining anything at all in linguistics'.[3]

Moreover, the very nature of language behaviour is still controversial. Its origin will forever remain a mystery, accessible only through myths. We still do not know exactly when or how human beings developed speech. We still do not know whether or not all languages are derived from the same 'mother tongue'.[4] What we do know is that the *speaker* or language-user is above all a social being; s/he was for a long time excluded from linguistics, but was finally allowed back in by the sociolinguists. This has led to a drastic redefinition of the subject matter of the science over the last quarter of a century and to still more controversy.

There is, however, a common denominator to all approaches to language: the aim of linguistics is to attempt to describe how *natural languages* work,

---

[3] Godzich (1974).

[4] The idea that all languages stem from the same 'Mother tongue' (whether God-given or not) was an object of speculation and debate for centuries until the advent of modern linguistics in the late 19th cent. (see Yaguello 1991). It has recently resurfaced in the work of Stanford scholars Joseph Greenberg and Merritt Ruhlen and of a school of Russian linguists. But they have failed so far to convince the linguistics community at large.

to point out the universal characteristics of *human language* and formulate hypotheses concerning the mysterious operations the human brain carries out in order to enable us to speak.

I am certainly not presuming to correct the haziness, or to resolve the contradictions. I simply propose to answer a question which has already been raised by numerous linguists in a fragmented, disorganized way, but for which nobody, to my knowledge, has provided a full, overarching answer: what does wordplay—in the broadest sense, including all language use which is not exclusively referential—teach us about language, its functions, its characteristics, its structure, and how it works?

I have taken from Carroll the idea of exploiting everything which falls within the area of *play* and *deviant use* (whether deliberate or not: I include slips of the tongue, for example), in order to describe the structures of a particular *language system* and work back from these, to the universal characteristics of human language. From time to time I will highlight a distinction that must be drawn between jokes about *language* (which are based on the *code*) and jokes about *content* (based on the *situation* to which the utterance refers): 'In order to understand wordplay and what it reveals about the code, we must draw on our knowledge of the *grammatical* features of the terms used in the joke, such as they have been set out elsewhere by linguists and grammarians.'[5]

So, in the end, the reader will learn from this book no more than s/he already knew, but never knew s/he knew.

The vast majority of examples in the chapters which follow are taken from English. And I should like to take advantage of this fact to refute a prejudice which is widely held, even by those who are well informed about language issues, that some languages are better suited to puns and wordplay and that some ethnic groups, accordingly, are wittier or sharper. This is simply not true. All languages allow play. Obviously, the linguistic features (syntactic, morphological, phonological, and prosodic) on which that play relies are distributed differently: this is why translation of wordplay is such a challenge.

Cultures differ in the social values attached to different forms of verbal activity. Depending on the culture, wordplay, verbal folklore, and poetry either are or are not given value as art forms. But the possibility of playing on and with words is universal.

---

[5] This view is elaborated on by Judith Milner (1976: 190).

1 What Language is For

Before considering how language is structured and how it works, we need to ask ourselves—as with any tool—what language is used for. The answer seems self-evident: language is for communication. But, for human beings, communicating is never merely a question of conveying information. Often we talk for the sake of talking, or we say the opposite of what we mean, or say something the addressee already knows. A good deal of the information we convey, moreover, is implicit: that is, it is absent from the message itself. Indeed, people speak for all sorts of reasons which have nothing to do with the act of informing: in order, for instance, to emphasize a position of power or to establish a relation of solidarity. The spoken word is not only a tool, but also a means of self-expression, a form of action, a way of asserting one-self as a social being, and a locus of pleasure or suffering.

Every act of verbal communication brings into play a *speaker*, who addresses a *message* to a hearer or *addressee* (who may be absent or implicit). The message has a *referent*: this is the subject matter of the discourse, what it refers to. Then, in order to construct the message, the speaker draws on a *code* (i.e. a language), which the addressee is assumed to share. Finally, communication requires the use of a physical *channel*—voice, writing, gesture, etc.—which serves to establish *contact*. These six features are closely interdependent in any speech act, but one or two may assume special prominence in particular kinds of communication.

The Functions of Language[1]

Six essential language functions emerge from the six features outlined above.

The *speaker* is associated with the **expressive** function conveying *emotion*.
The *addressee* is associated with the **conative** function conveying *commands*.
The *referent* is associated with the **informative** function conveying *information*.

---

[1] This presentation of the functions of language is adapted from Roman Jakobson's famous essay 'Linguistics and poetics', first published in Sebeok (1960).

The *channel* is associated with the **phatic** function conveying *communion*.
The *code* is associated with the **metalinguistic** function conveying *code analysis*.
The *message* is associated with the **poetic** function conveying *play, pleasure*.

As I have already hinted, an utterance does not necessarily come under the heading of one function alone. More often than not, several functions overlap: utterances are classified on the basis of the dominant function. Except in a few radical poetic experiments—such as sound poetry, which pares language down to the level of pure sound substance—the message is very seldom totally devoid of any referential value, even if it is clearly of subsidiary importance, as is the case in wordplay, rhymes and so on. Similarly, when you say 'ouch!', you are clearly articulating the expressive function. But at the same time you are also informing the people around you that you are in pain (informative function). Or again, when you sing the praises of a product in an advertisement, you are seeking not only to inform consumers but also to give the message more impact, make it more amusing (poetic function), while also trying to induce a certain type of behaviour (conative function). It is not, then, a matter of sorting out the functions, so much as assessing their relative importance in a given utterance.

Who Says What to Whom?

Each of the first three functions in the list above emphasizes in turn the speaker, the addressee, or the referent of the message. We find a correlation here with the three corners of the triangle formed by the grammatical 'persons' (see Figure 1.1).

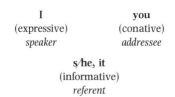

FIG. 1.1. The grammatical 'persons'

But there is a basic dissymmetry in this triangular relationship: the first and second persons are interdependent, as components of the *utterance situation*:

I [the speaker] am saying (this) to *you* [the addressee].

The first and second person are not necessarily expressed overtly in the message, although they can always be reintroduced into a discourse for purposes of clarification as in 'Who said that?': 'I did'; or 'Who are you talking to?': 'Why you, of course'.

This leaves the third person as the odd one out. It is only a component of the utterance proper; that is, of what is actually said.

(I) am saying *something* to (you) about *him/her/it*.

While the *referent* of the third person can always be found within the *verbal context*, the referents of the first and second persons can only be assigned within the *speech situation*. *I* and *you* are peculiar in that they have no other meaning than 'the person speaking' and 'the person being spoken to'. They are 'empty' words to which only the speech situation can give a meaning. *I* and *you* are the only 'true' persons, in the literal sense of the word. The third person is, in fact, a *non-person*, a way of designating the topic, what is being talked about, nothing more. It may be human or non-human, animate or inanimate, real or imaginary, concrete or abstract. And the third person can appear in one of a very large variety of guises: personal or demonstrative pronouns (which in some languages can vary between *masculine* and *feminine*, *animate* and *inanimate*, *human* and *non-human*, *near* and *far*, or a combination of these features), verb endings if no pronoun is used,[2] proper or common nouns, and so on.

I and *you* alternate during dialogue and for this reason are called *shifters*. An anecdote from Jewish folklore illustrates this aspect of communication. A man writes to his friend:

Dear Riwke, be good enough to send me your slippers. Of course, I mean 'my slippers' and not 'your slippers'. But, if you read 'my slippers', you will think I mean your slippers. Whereas, if I write: 'send me your slippers', you will read *your* slippers and will understand that I want *my* slippers. So: send me your slippers.[3]

The story points up a genuine difficulty. It is well known that for children the appropriation of the *I*, which allows the child to take on the role of speaker and enter into intersubjective communication, comes quite late in the language acquisition process. For a long time the child continues to speak of itself in the third person (a habit which persists—incidentally—in some forms of mental illness). In the same way, we can all remember that when Jane addresses Tarzan—'You Tarzan, me Jane'—he has great difficulty in responding correctly—'You Jane, me Tarzan', in other words in 'shifting' the pronouns. The use of the third person is also the norm in strip cartoon dialogues and films portraying the speech of 'natives', a fact reflecting the prejudiced view that 'developed' cultures have of the supposedly infantile mentality of such peoples.

---

[2] As is the case in Latin, Spanish, Italian, and the Slavic languages.
[3] Cf. J. Milner (1976).

Q: What is it that is always coming but never arrives?

A: Tomorrow. When it arrives, it is today.

So goes the riddle. Adverbs of time and space are also shifters. Thus, the reference of *yesterday*, *today*, and *tomorrow*, *here* and *there*, can only be worked out in relation to the speaker's *co-ordinates*—the time and place of utterance—which are endlessly moving on. When the Queen suggests that Alice become her chambermaid, in exchange for which Alice shall have jam 'every other day', Alice declines the offer, arguing that she does not want any jam *today*. 'You couldn't have it', answers the Queen, 'if you *did* want it. . . . The rule is, jam tomorrow and jam yesterday—but never jam *to-day*.' Alice protests, 'It *must* come sometimes to "jam to-day".'[4] Alice clearly believes in the power of shifters, whereas it is precisely the rule which allows *tomorrow* to become *today* and *today* to become *yesterday*—or *I* to become *you* and *you* to become *I*—which the Queen is denying.

The three basic functions—expressive, conative, informative—can, in turn, be used to define three types of poetry:

(1) *Lyric*, in which the poet gives free rein to his/her feelings ('I wandered lonely as a cloud');

(2) *Elegiac*, which incites the reader to follow the poet ('Let us go then, you and I | When the evening is spread out against the sky');

(3) *Epic*, which tells of the great deeds of heroes ('Of Man's first disobedience . . . [s]ing, Heavenly Muse').

More generally, in literature, the narrator can be a part of the narrative (the first-person narrative), can address the readers—or one privileged reader—directly (as, for example, in Sterne's *Tristram Shandy*), or remain entirely outside the narrative (as in the so-called 'objective', naturalist or realist novel). A further process, consisting of the narrator addressing himself, as though addressing a double, has often been used by the French 'nouveaux romanciers', such as Michel Butor in *La Modification*, or Georges Perec, in his novel *Un homme qui dort*.[5] One of Alice's characteristics is to talk constantly to herself, either for encouragement, or to tell herself off:

'Come, there's no use in crying like that!' said Alice to herself, rather sharply; 'I advise you to leave off this minute!' (31)

---

[4] *Alice in Wonderland* (also containing *Through the Looking Glass*), Norton Critical Edition, ed. Donald J. Gray (London: W. W. Norton and Company, 1992), 150. This is the edition used throughout. Page references are given in parentheses after the quotation.

[5] *A Man Asleep*, trans. David Bellos.

Ego Tripping: The Expressive Function

Each different language function favours different grammatical and stylistic processes. The *expressive* function, for instance, involves the use of interjections, onomatopoeia, swear words, and exclamations. Captain Haddock, Tintin's companion in all of his adventures, is well known for proffering strings of very creative oaths and insults. Alice, for her part, is so polite that the only interjections she allows herself to use are 'well' or 'oh dear'.

© HERGÉ / MOULINSART 1998

'Well', thought Alice to herself, 'after such a fall as this, I shall think nothing of tumbling downstairs! How brave they'll all think me at home !' (25)

. . . 'But, oh dear!', cried Alice, with a sudden burst of tears, 'I do wish they would put their heads down! I'm so very tired of being all alone here!' (37)

Intonation also plays an important role in the expression of the emotions: joy, anger, surprise, suffering, enthusiasm, and so on. Such *paralinguistic* features as mimickry, gesture, mannerisms, speed of delivery, tone and volume of the voice, can all support and complement the message proper. Dostoyevsky, for example, in his *Diary of a Writer*, tells of a conversation between six tipsy workers outside a bar, who take it in turns to pronounce the single word 'Shit!', each of them giving it a totally different emotional— and referential—meaning.

Open, Sesame!: The Conative Function

The imperative mood, the use of various forms of address (socially codified for the most part) are specific to the *conative* function. They serve to create a link between the speaker and the addressee. In this way, relations which are external to the utterance proper—that is to say *pragmatic* relations—can be asserted.

The spoken word is actually a form of action, often fraught with ritualistic or magical significance. God said, in *The Bible*, 'Let there be light': and there was light. 'Abracadabra', 'Open, Sesame', religious or magical formulas, prayer: all reflect the conative function (even when addressed to an imaginary you). Here the important thing is that the speaker believes in the power of The Word over the addressee. A baby crying in order to get someone to come and look after it is also expressing this function. The child soon discovers the near magical effect of its crying on the people around it: one extreme example would be little Oscar, in *The Tin Drum* by Günther Grass, whose scream shatters glass. Or again, advertising or political posters, encouraging us to buy—a product, an ideology—make frequent use of *you*, pointing a finger at the targeted onlooker.

The conative function is also instantiated in a special category of verbs, called *speech-act verbs*, or performatives: these derive their meaning from the action which the speaker performs on the addressee simply by uttering them. The verbs are grounded in the action, not in the code. As with imperatives, performative predicates are unusual in that their truth cannot be challenged. When someone says, 'I baptize you', for example, or 'I pronounce you man and wife', 'I declare you elected', 'Arise, Sir John', or 'Sold!', the words embody an act, stand for that act: what we are witnessing in such cases is a codified ceremony which assumes a legally binding force (provided, of course, that the person speaking is qualified to perform the duty in question). If there is any pretence or play, the performative is emptied of its meaning, as in the trial of the playing cards at the end of *Alice's Adventures in Wonderland*.

Thus the conative function is expressed in any act of communication which transforms or attempts to transform reality or people, which aims to affect the course of events or the behaviour of individuals.

Elephants Have Right of Way: The Informative Function

Utterances with purely utilitarian value can be considered as strictly referential: 'Road Closed', 'This Side Up', or this amazing sign tourists may see in African game reserves: 'ELEPHANTS HAVE RIGHT OF WAY'! Other examples are telegrams—in which every single word carries information—or scientific and technical texts, from which any expressive or aesthetic intention has been removed.

As often as not, however, the informative function co-exists with others: while it may be the job of information science to stock and manipulate information in its purest, most rudimentary form, *human* language is never completely neutral. Whatever we say, we usually say more than we mean to say.

Nice Weather for the Time of Year!: The Phatic Function

The phatic function (a word coined by the Polish anthropologist Malinowski) maintains *contact* between speakers and ensures the smooth operation of the channel of communication.

This function already exists prior to articulate language, since the babbling noises made by a new-born baby enable it to establish contact with those around it, while also reassuring its carers about the normality of its speech organs. Indeed, it is well known that without such contact the baby actually stops making the noises: it is of vital importance to speak to babies, so as not to jeopardize their linguistic, emotional, and social development. Given this socializing function of language, play and contact are essential and take precedence over information.

In what is called *mediated* communication—by telephone, radio, etc.—all sorts of fixed expressions are available to check the 'circuit': 'Hello, can you hear me?', or 'Receiving you loud and clear', 'Roger'. The speech of a teacher, too, includes numerous interruptions intended to check that attention does not flag and to ensure understanding: 'Do you follow?', 'Do you see what I mean?', 'Listen carefully', 'Let me repeat that', and so on. In the same way, our conversations are riddled with automatic occurrences of 'you see' and 'you know'.

Listeners for their part use phatic words such as 'I see', 'oh dear!', 'right!', 'really?' to convey their appreciation or to signal attention to what the speaker is saying. This kind of feedback is essential in face to face communication and even more so on the telephone.

Finally, in our everyday lives, many exchanges aim only to initiate or maintain social contact. When, for example, a driver picks up a hitch-hiker, one or the other invariably feels obliged to strike up a conversation which by and large is an exchange of banalities, simply because silence in this kind of situation is usually interpreted as hostility. We find the same motivation in most cocktail-party conversations or 'small talk'. In Western society the rule is that we talk when in company, for the sake of talking, and it is only in certain situations (our dealings with our nearest and dearest, very formal relationships, or at work) that we can keep quiet if we have nothing to say. During a dinner party, a pregnant pause will cause general embarrassment and a carefully maintained stock of anecdotes and funny stories is the usual way of keeping up verbal contact without a break. Some people feel genuine panic when contact is broken, because it means that everyone is left to their own devices. And we all know people who endlessly restart the conversation on the doorstep when they are about to leave.

One of the most interesting aspects of *Alice in Wonderland* is that it challenges the phatic function. Alice finds herself in a rather disconcerting world, where the different characters show the highest disregard for *phatic communication*. The rules of conversation as practised in the real world are constantly derided and their stereotyped nature underlined. Polite expressions, sentences or phrases meant to establish or maintain contact, are all taken literally or deliberately misconstrued:

'Oh, I'm not particular as to size', Alice hastily replied; 'Only one doesn't like changing so often, you know.'

'I *don't* know', said the Caterpillar. (71)

'Goodbye, till we meet again!', [Alice] said as cheerfully as she could. 'I shouldn't know you again if we did meet', Humpty Dumpty replied in a discontented tone. (168)

There is no room in Wonderland, it would appear, for automatic language.

The Word 'Dog' does not Bark: The Metalinguistic Function

'Edwin and Morcar, the earls of Mercia and Northumbria, declared for [William the Conqueror]: and even Stignand, the patriotic Archbishop of Canterbury, found it advisable—'
'Found *what?*' said the Duck.
'Found *it*', the Mouse replied rather crossly. 'Of course you know what "it" means.'
'I know what "it" means well enough, when *I* find a thing', said the Duck. 'It's generally a frog or a worm. The question is, what did the Archbishop find?' (22)

What Carroll is exploiting here is the fact that a word—in this case the pronoun *it*—can either be *used* or *mentioned* in an utterance. The first occurrence of *it* refers to an element in the verbal context, announcing the infinitive clause which follows (even if the Duck does interpret *it* wrongly). In the second case, *it* is auto-referential, designating only the word 'it'; this is a metalinguistic use, which is consequently pointed up in the text by inverted commas or italics (which would correspond to a slight pause when spoken).[6] The same opposition is exploited in child wordplay in 'Where Simon had had had had, Peter had had had'. Once punctuated the sentence reads more easily: 'Where Simon had had "had had", Peter had had "had".'

Now take the following sentence:

(1) The dog is barking.

If we were to perform a grammatical analysis of the sentence, we would say:

(2) *The dog* is the subject of the verb *is barking.*

The dog then has as its referent the phrase 'the dog' and no longer, as in (1), a particular dog which you could point to. Hence the principle which sums up the metalinguistic function: the word *dog* does not bark.

Language alone, of all sign systems, is endowed with the power of *self-interpretation*, to use Émile Benveniste's term. Language, alone, can talk about itself and all other codes. Language, alone, can take itself as object of analysis and establish a circular, reflexive relationship. Among the six lan-

---

[6] Generally speaking inverted commas have metalinguistic value, sometimes even when a word is being used rather than mentioned. Inverted commas (or 'scare quotes') are a way of showing that the speaker/writer is distancing himself/herself from the word and is thereby taking up a position in respect of its linguistic value, its place in the system. It may be that the word constitutes a non-lexicalized figure of speech, or a neologism, a rather bold or unexpected use of the term, a word borrowed from a foreign language or a slang term, or one which is too familiar for the context.

guage functions, therefore, the metalinguistic function must be given a prominent place. Indeed, the *expressive, conative,* and *phatic* functions are not peculiar to language and can be expressed through behaviour, mimickry, or gesture. As for the informative function, it can be taken on by various other sign systems, such as graphic or ideographic codes (which is more and more the case for information of an international nature as in airports and stations), or mimickry—as resorted to by the traveller lost in a foreign country. The *poetic* function, to which we shall return later, can be seen as part of a broader aesthetic function including all forms of artistic expression. Only the *metalinguistic* function is inseparable from language, since it is focused on the code and how the code works.

A good deal of metalinguistic activity is unconscious. It underlies all language activity. Although it is made conscious when one learns a foreign language or explores one's native language in a systematic way at school, the activity is clearly unconscious in the child learning its mother tongue. It is partly conscious in speakers whenever they make language choices: stylistic choices, finding the 'right' word, in word games, punning, crosswords, anagrams, or any other game requiring the analysis of the meaning or function of words. In order to complete a crossword, for example, one needs a thorough knowledge of the workings of *synonymy, homonymy, polysemy,* and the ambiguities they generate and, therefore, of the figures of speech—metaphor, metonymy, transferred epithet—which are often responsible for that ambiguity.

Unconscious metalinguistic activity is apparent in a child learning to speak, since it often produces *neologisms* quite spontaneously, thereby showing that it has mastered the principle of analogy. It is in this sense that we can say that a child's 'mistakes'—*goed* instead of *went, taked* instead of *took,* or *putted* for *put*—are in practice evidence of the development of its linguistic competence, illustrating the child's acquisition of the rule for forming the simple past tense of regular verbs.

In aphasics who are affected by a similarity disorder, the metalinguistic function is impaired. Such speakers lose all capacity for metaphor,[7] or the comparison of terms which are equivalent in their function or meaning. They are therefore incapable of organizing words into syntactic classes or semantic fields, they cannot paraphrase an utterance, translate it into another language or transpose it into another system of signs—for example, by putting into words the information on road traffic signs.

The whole of the famous dialogue between Alice and Humpty Dumpty, in chapter 6 of *Through the Looking-Glass,* is metalinguistic in nature. Humpty Dumpty gives Alice a lesson in semantics, first interpreting the poem *Jabberwocky,* the words of which were coined by Lewis Carroll (see below,

---

[7] Cf. Jakobson (1941).

Chapter 9), then setting out his own theory on the arbitrary nature of the sign (see Chapter 8). 'Arbitrary', for Humpty, takes its strict etymological sense of 'free will', the will and whim of the language-user—which is clearly not the meaning of the word in linguistics. For Humpty, the speaker has the power to make words mean exactly what s/he likes. Words are therefore reduced to being the servants of a master, albeit a benevolent one: 'When I make a word do a lot of work . . . I always pay it extra' (164).

The Obscure Object of Desire: The Poetic Function

> O mouths, Man is searching for a new language
> Which no grammarian will have anything to say about
> The old languages are so close to death
> That it is only by force of habit or want of courage
> That we still make use of them for poetry.
>
> (Guillaume Apollinaire)

Human beings have a relationship of an erotic nature with language. Language is an object of love, and a source of pleasure.[8] A child's natural tendency is towards play, disorder, pleasure, freedom, and creative imagination. This tendency is thwarted, during the child's socialization process, by an increasing realization of the rules—both structural and social—which govern language and language use. The child has to learn to speak like grown-ups in order to be understood and integrated into the linguistic community. The reality principle, which progressively supplants the pleasure principle, also manifests itself in the tough realities of learning the code, as well as the correlate of that: the *mistake*, which is somehow seen as akin to a moral fault. At the babbling stage, language is simply music for the child, a purely gratuitous game, which then gradually acquires its utilitarian value for communication. But, for a long time, language remains a game, unbridled exploration, sheer pleasure.

Playing with words—sounds or meaning—any activity which has language as both subject matter and as means of expression, constitutes the survival of the pleasure principle, preserving the gratuitous in the face of the utilitarian. Play is within language and *vice versa*, since humankind is, basically, made for playing. After all, humans copulate, but eroticism is a game. Humans need to eat, but cooking is an art. Humans speak to communicate, but speaking is also a form of play.

The word 'play' in English has (at least) the following meanings:

as a verb

(1) to take part in a game;

---

[8] See Jean-Claude Milner (1978) and Wolfson (1970).

(2) to perform;
(3) to engage in activity for amusement;
as a noun
(4) rule-governed activity;
(5) a text for performance;
(6) leeway, latitude, freedom.

This gives us two apparently contradictory sets of meanings. On the one hand, there is the idea of elasticity, freedom, leeway and, on the other, the idea of rules or constraints. Indeed, it is a defining feature of play that it combines unruliness with rules, freedom with limits.[9] There are constraints placed on language, yet if we could take no liberties with it, it would merely be a mechanical code. Only formal or artificial languages forbid play. Language has a certain play in it, in the same way we might say there is *play* in a mechanism or a structure. And, if play is, above all, a way of distancing oneself from something, then playing with words is a way of distancing oneself from language and, therefore, from oneself. The inability to play with words reveals an ontological shortcoming.

Language is a game (a structure) whose rules are frequently bent. It allows all kinds of cheating and hitting below the belt and it is quite impossible to define precisely the overall scope of what is allowed and what is not. And yet, neither can it be said—since there are rules—that absolutely *anything* is allowed (see Chapter 10). Language carries within itself the possibility of its own subversion or sabotage. This is what makes Jakobson (1973) say: 'To the theory which holds that verse corresponds to the spirit of language, we can oppose the theory that the poetic form commits organized violence on language.'

'Language has been given to man to make surrealist use of it', said André Breton in *Le manifeste surréaliste*.[10] Clearly Lewis Carroll, Edward Lear, and many others also felt that words were made to be played with. If Eros and Thanatos are connected, it is understandable that love of language should make poets want to destructure it to its utmost limits, even to murder it. This is what Joyce or Gertrude Stein do, or the French surrealist writer and dramatist Antonin Artaud—for whom 'all real language is incomprehensible'. Love of language also motivates extremist experiments like Dadaism or lettrism. I deal with these extreme aspects of language use in Chapters 9 and 11.

Play is also a revolt against clichés, linguistic redundancy, and stereotypes, against all forms of mechanical, thoughtless, meaningless language use. Deliberate nonsense—as practised by Edward Lear for instance—is always preferable to meaninglessness.

---

[9] See Huizinga (1951).   [10] Translated into English as *The Surrealist Manifesto*.

A basic distinction can be drawn between two types of game: playing with form—spoken or written—and playing with meaning (as well, of course, as playing with both at the same time). 'In poetry', writes Jakobson (1973), 'every apparent similarity of sound, is treated in terms of similarity and/or difference of meaning.' But we should not restrict form to sound because many games also exploit the graphic dimension of written language.

Playing with sound is comprised essentially of rhyme, repetition, alliteration (repetition of consonants), assonance (repetition of vowels), the juxtaposition or substitution of paronyms (words which are phonetically very similar as in rhyming slang), misdivisions, and spoonerisms.

Playing with meaning comprises the unexpected juxtaposition of words which are quite unlike each other, or the artful exploitation of synonymy, all forms of ambiguity, deliberate violations of meaning—'Sethe looked down at her feet again and saw the sycamores' (Toni Morrison)—corruption and allusion.

These processes are found not only in poetry as such, but also in proverbs, aphorisms, and language-games of schoolchildren: in nursery rhymes, skipping or clapping songs. Children start playing with sound before they start playing with meaning. After a purely sensual stage, during which the child derives pleasure from repeating the sounds, it moves on to a more intellectual stage where meaning becomes increasingly dominant. One only has to observe, in the verbal behaviour of children aged between about 6 and 12, the importance of riddles and language games which set 'traps'. The same processes—corruption, allusion, paronymic progression, etc.—are also found in magical and ritual formulas, commercial and political slogans, book and film titles, and so on. For the poetic function is not limited to the field of poetry; it encompasses all verbal production—whether improvised or carefully prepared, rooted in tradition or ephemeral—in which is found an arrangement of sound and meaning meant to focus attention on the form of the message, regardless of its content or communicative aim.

Here are a few examples:

Paronymic progressions

> There once was a fisher named Fisher
> Who fished for a fish in a fissure
> But the fish with a grin
> Pulled the fisherman in
> Now they all fish the fissure for Fisher

Slogans

These draw on paronymy, parallelism, repetition, rhyme and alliteration:

> Clunk, click, every trip (a reminder to put on seat belts)
> Kids cook quick (protect your children from the sun!)

Up yours, Delors (British press against EC federalism)
Hatch, Match and Dispatch ('Births, Marriages, Deaths')
Three tenors for under a tenner (opera advertisement)
Ninteresting Nincentive Nintendo (computer game)
Check out our new check in (Airline advertisement)

Corruption and allusion are both highly prized:

Beauty and the piste (winter holiday advertisement)
A dedicated follower of function (Mercedes advertisement)
Merchant of venison (Sunday supplement cookery page)
All pomp and no circumstance (on lacklustre football match)
Fat and fiction (advertisement for margarine)

as are stylistic features and the ambiguity allowed by polysemic words:

Labour isn't working (Conservative election slogan)
France: discover a land of placid valleys, rocky gorges and mountainous lunches.

Biblical sayings
These are also often subject to the law of parallelism:[11]

An eye for an eye and a tooth for a tooth
The spirit is willing, but the flesh is weak

as are

Proverbs

Like father, like son
He who laughs last, laughs longest
Once a thief always a thief
All's well that ends well
What's good for the goose is good for the gander
Take care of the pounds and the pence will take care of themselves

and

Children's rhymes

Finding's keeping
Taking back's stealing.

Giveses, keepses.
Finders keepers
Losers weepers.

Touch wood, no good
Touch iron, rely on.

---

[11] See Jousse (1978).

Cross my heart and hope to die
Drop down dead if I tell a lie.

Book titles

These make use of the same processes—repetition, paronymy, corruption, allusion, polysemy:

Absalom, Absalom!
Antic Hay
Arms and the Man
Endgame
Erewhon
Eyeless in Gaza
Language Through the Looking-Glass
Tinker, Tailor, Soldier, Spy
Where Angels Fear to Tread

as do

Newspaper headlines

The merchant of venom (about a politician from Venice)
Star tekkies (high-tech design and architecture in Britain)
Saddling up for the future (about plans for rebuilding Sadler's Wells)
A marriage maid in heaven (about submissive oriental wives)
Day of the long knives (about a cookery competition)

and

Nursery rhymes

eeny, meeny, miny, mo
fee, fi, fo, fum

It should be noted that 'baby talk' makes spontaneous use of rhyme and repetition. At the babbling stage words are naturally binary: all languages have equivalents of: *bye-bye, choo-choo, din-dins, gee-gee, poo-poo, tum-tum, wee-wee*, etc., which correspond, according to certain psychoanalysts, to an urge to repeat. In the vocabulary of adults, words with affectionate connotations, are often experienced as an infantile regression towards an original binary rhythm: *coodgy-coodgy, lovey-dovey*, or the rather more evocative *rumpy-pumpy*. This is why the language linked to play and pleasure is often found in lovemaking.

But rhymed words are by no means restricted to child or childlike language; adult speakers use words such as *chit-chat, dilly-dally, helter-skelter, hocus-pocus, hotch-potch, mish-mash, riff-raff, willy-nilly, wishy-washy*, and so on. These words, whether through assonance or alliteration, are peculiar in that they defy analysis (see Chapter 5) and offer a meaning and a resonance which are playful, or in any event frivolous. Frozen in the lexis of the language, they constitute a reminder of the natural tendency of speakers to play with sound.

What separates poetry proper from language used in such things as slogans is the absolute pre-eminence of the poetic over the referential or the conative. In slogans, the poetic function is only a superficial phenomenon, a means to an end, even if the formal processes are the same. On the other hand, what separates poetry from pure play is the communicative aim which persists in the poetic text. Poetry which was merely formal play, which evoked *nothing*, would be singularly limited (see Chapter 9).

Another important distinction can be made between spontaneous, free, creative play (poetry, wordplay, punning, etc.) and rule-governed play (anagrams, crosswords, *Scrabble*, etc.), which aims to impose order. In the same way, two stages can be distinguished in children: that of free, unconstrained play and a second, later stage, of rule-governed play which is part of the socialization process, since play—paradoxically—can be defined as both subversion of the social norm and integration into it.

In some societies verbal play is given very high status: such societies encourage and value such ritual manifestations of language as *verbal duelling*, or *verbal jousting, talking in riddles,* and *ritual insults*. Verbal duelling, a ritual confrontation in words, as practised for example among pre-adolescent Turks, demands virtuosity in the art of linking and rhyming repartee and insults. It amounts to a rite of passage, an initiation which gives access to the world of grown men. Among the young Blacks of the American inner cities the practice of ritual insults—*dozens* or *sounding*—which accompanies their adolescent years, allows them to let off steam.[12] It is a substitute for aggression and also demands virtuoso manipulation of the language: rhymes, puns, double-meanings, and figures of speech follow each other at breakneck speed. The rule is that what one says should have no link with reality, so the informative function is totally ignored. The use of riddles, which in our culture is restricted to schoolchildren, is also highly valued in many societies with an oral culture. In Madagascar, where language games are considered the supreme art form, verbal jousting, or *hain-teny* can go on for days at a time in front of fascinated audiences. By contrast, we in the West are increasingly buried beneath the mass of the referential, of the purely, merely informational and the utilitarian. Poets and word-jugglers have lost the pre-eminent place in the city which was formerly reserved for them.

[12] Cf. Labov (1972b).

2 The Tower of Babel
Universal Characteristics of Language

Language is something all human beings share. There is no difference of *nature* between languages, only structural differences. Nor are there any 'simple' or 'complex' languages: they are all equally simple and equally complex. A language may have a simple morphology and a complex syntax . . . or the other way around. The so-called 'theory of stages', which sought to establish a hierarchy of languages, from the *primitive* up to the *developed* stage, according to the degree of 'civilization' of their speakers, was refuted a long time ago.[1]

All natural languages have in common certain universal properties, or characteristics which can be used to define what human language is. For, beyond the extraordinary *diversity* of the languages spoken in the world, we need to recognize the fundamental *unity* of human language, what is specific to it as compared with non-human codes of communication. Humankind has always been aware of this, if only at a mythical level. It could even be argued that the myth of the Tower of Babel (the biblical explanation for the diversity of languages) and the nostalgia for the lost paradise of the single, primeval, pre-Babel language, find their echo in the contemporary search for language universals, the mental operations which underlie the workings of all languages.[2]

To begin with, there are two features which we usually take for granted. First, a linguistic message is *linear*—something which distinguishes it from a musical message, for example, which allows notes to be superimposed on each other (plain chant treats the voice as an instrument). Second, linguistic units are *discrete*, that is they can be distinguished from one another—something which the blank spaces in writing point up. While the colour spectrum, for instance, constitutes a continuum whose divisions are arbitrarily drawn by language, a linguistic message is a sequence of distinct units, however much they appear to be run together in normal speech. These two properties—linearity and discreteness—are what makes it possible to break messages down, to analyse them.

All languages include *redundancy* (an excess of means relative to the information actually transmitted) and this is the topic of Chapter 3.

---

[1] Cf. Yaguello (1991*b*).   [2] Ibid.

All languages show a double articulation in units of meaning (words or morphemes) and units of sound (vowels and consonants or phonemes). These two kinds of units are discussed in detail in Chapters 4 to 6.

All languages are systems whose units are defined in relation to the system as a whole, as organized by its overall structure. The relationship between sound and meaning is *arbitrary*, i.e. conventional. I will take up these points in Chapters 7 and 8.

Languages also display *ambiguity, synonymy, polysemy, dissymmetry*, and *irregularity* as will be seen in Chapters 5 and 14.

Languages are all structured at three different levels: *sound, grammatical arrangement, meaning* (see Chapters 9 to 11). They can all, beginning from a theoretically *finite* number of signs, generate an infinite number of utterances (see Chapter 10). They all allow *invention, creativity, shifts of meaning, play*, and the use of *stylistic devices* (see Chapters 11 to 13).

Finally, languages are all, by nature, in constant evolution, which is a sign of vitality rather than of decay. A language that does not change any more is a language that is about to die.[3]

In the chapters which follow, we shall be looking in turn at each of the characteristics mentioned in the paragraphs above. But I shall also emphasize the fact that since language is organized as a multi-level, interconnected system, each concept is linked to all the others and the decision to treat them in sequence is necessarily, to an extent, an arbitrary decision.

---

[3] And this indeed happens more and more often, as languages gradually fall out of use and disappear. The number of human languages in use is rapidly decreasing. Estimates of the rate of disappearance vary from 12 to 50 per year. This means that up to 10 per cent of the linguistic heritage of humankind will be irretrievably lost by 2005. By the end of the 21st cent., it is estimated that less than 1,000 of the present 5,000+ languages will still be in existence. Linguists are increasingly aware that the threatened languages must be documented before it is too late.

3 Pink Elephants
Redundancy at Work

> The elephant is a pretty bird
> It flies from bough to bough
> It builds its nest in a rhubarb tree
> And whistles like a cow

Do you know how to play 'Crash'? I choose a word and you choose another one with the same number of letters: five, say. I try to guess yours and you try to guess mine. To do this, each of us takes turns at suggesting five-letter words and the other says how many correct letters—from none to five—the word contains. Once I guess the first letter, it is simple enough to guess the others, provided I change only one letter at a time in each successive word I suggest.

When playing this game, it soon becomes clear that consonants are much more helpful and provide much more information than vowels, which can easily be worked out from the context formed by the consonants. To a considerable extent we can predict what the vowels are going to be,[1] whereas the opposite is not the case. As a result, we can say that the information conveyed by consonants and vowels is proportional to their number in the alphabet. Generally speaking, there are more consonants in a language than vowels[2]—a difference which is made more obvious in the written language. In English, only five *written* vowels (a, e, i, o, u) are used to represent 20 vocalic *sounds* (see Chapter 6, Figure 6.1).

What is equally relevant is the way sounds (or letters) are combined. Certain clusters of sounds or letters are especially frequent and, because of this, provide relatively little information. Others, on the contrary, are rare and consequently highly informative. But let's get back to our game. Suppose you have chosen the word *tweet*. If I guess the two vowels, I shall still have quite a lot of work to do in order to win the game, since the number of five-letter words containing *ee* in this position is very large. If, on the

[1] This is what allows written Hebrew, for example, to dispense with the vowels. In any language, in fact, it is the vowels which are the least stable sounds in the process of phonetic change.

[2] It would seem that the smallest number of vowels is three and the largest number of consonants around 80. English is about average, since the number of consonant phonemes (24) is only slightly greater than the vowel phonemes (20).

other hand, I guess the *w*, I know that only *d*, *s*, and *t* can come before *w*. When I have suggested *swell* or *dwell*, for example, there only remains the combination *tw*, which begins fewer than ten words in English, among which only *tweet* and *tweed* form a pair distinguished by a single consonant. And there we are, I have all but won.

Some players choose words containing an unusual cluster of letters. But this cuts both ways. True, my opponent might not immediately think of a word ending in *fth*, for example, but once s/he guesses that, the rest is plain sailing. By the same token, it soon becomes clear that it is easier to guess the end of a word from the beginning than the other way around: that is, the beginning is more helpful, provides more information than the end.

When playing Crash, then, we are working from a knowledge of the combinations of letters which are licensed by the structure of the language and its spelling system: an oral version of the game could equally well be played, but would use different rules of combination, because of the discrepancy between spoken and written English. In practice, the player of a game like Crash is discovering, by trial and error, that principle of information theory called *redundancy*: the more predictable it is that a given element will appear in a given context, the less information that element provides and the more redundant it is.

Among other things, redundancy allows us to abbreviate words. In the written language we omit vowels rather than consonants—with the exception of initial vowels—and we clip the end of a word rather than the beginning. For example: *adj., adv., all mod. cons., attn., aux., des.res., spag.bol., 2 receps., 2 beds., ftd. cpts., recap., vb.* In the spoken language, it is impossible, of course, to leave out the vowels, since they form the basis of all pronunciation—you cannot have a syllable without a vowel sound. But we do readily omit the end of a word which can be worked out from the context: the more so since most long words end in a suffix. For example, we say *demo* for *demonstration, Eng lit* for *English literature, fab* for *fabulous, fax* for *facsimile, lib* for *liberation, met* for *metropolitan, pub* for *public house, vet* for *veterinary*. But it is possible to cut off the beginning of the word, too, as in *bus, phone, plane, loo*, and so on: or both the beginning and the end, as in *flu*.

The way we abbreviate words tells us a lot about the structure of syllables. In English, a language in which syllables tend to be closed—that is, ending in a consonant—words are often truncated after a consonant. In French, the opposite tends to be true, since it has predominantly open syllables. English, in general, abbreviates rather less than French: English words are, by and large, shorter than words in the Romance languages and therefore exhibit less redundancy. Where abbreviations do exist they may become fully lexicalized, e.g. *bike, cab, flu, mike, plane, telly, vibes, zoo*. These, and others, have become words in their own right. Who remembers now that *mob* was an eighteenth-century abbreviation of the Latin expression *mobile vulgus?*

All languages have redundant elements at every level, elements which provide little or no information at all. They can be found at the level of the possible sound combinations, in the letters used to transcribe them, in the combinations of syllables used to form words and the combinations of words used to form groups of words and sentences. Redundant elements are often distributed differently in different languages, but redundancy as a linguistic feature is always present in a consistent proportion. Telegrams, headlines, and advertising slogans draw on the redundancy of certain grammatical features: these types of message emphasize the elements in an utterance which are the most heavily laden with meaning, to the detriment of those which, being predictable, can easily be left out. Hence, the verb *to be*—which, indeed, does not even exist in many languages—is highly redundant. Similarly, articles, pronouns and prepositions are more or less redundant, insofar as they can be deduced from the context. The systematic agreement in gender and number which many languages require (the Slavic and Romance languages, for example) is very obviously redundant: in French, when we say *la petite chatte*, the feminine is indicated three times.

The same is true of set expressions, linguistic stereotypes, clichés, idioms, and collocations where one word automatically calls up another—*mad as a . . . hatter, good as . . . gold*, and so on. Redundancy of this kind is a feature of 'bad' literature and a poetic text is precisely that text which thwarts redundancy by associating words in an unexpected way. Pink elephants are less redundant than grey ones. If you wear tennis shoes with a dinner jacket or a swimsuit with a top hat, you will have more chance of being noticed than if you wore the same footwear with a sports outfit, or the same headgear with morning dress.

We have to struggle against the force of habit:

> A tail behind, a trunk in front,
> Complete the usual elephant.
> The tail in front, the trunk behind,
> Is what you very seldom find.
> If you for specimens should hunt,
> With trunks behind and tails in front,
> That hunt would occupy you long;
> the force of habit is so strong.[3]

But redundancy is there for a reason. It has a precise function: to make communication easier when conditions are poor—on the telephone, over the radio, in a noisy environment. It saves having to pay constant attention, whether speaking or listening, or having to wrestle with certain forms of

---

[3] A. E. Housman, *The Elephant, or The Force of Habit.*

ambiguity and it helps us avoid misunderstandings. In short, it saves us having to counter all forms of interference; what communication theory refers to as 'noise'. If the level of 'noise' or jamming is too high, redundancy is defeated. This is well illustrated in the game known as 'Chinese Whispers': a general sends out a distress call to HQ, 'Send reinforcements, we are going to advance'. The message, passed on from soldier to soldier, arrives at length at its destination: 'Send three and fourpence, we are going to a dance.'[4] Here, redundancy has finally met its match.

Redundancy has yet another function. Within a sentence, grammatical agreement, such as the repetition of gender or number in nouns, pronouns, and adjectives, or concord between a subject and a verb, help us to identify which words belong together and what grammatical function they assume.

Redundancy allows us to obviate mistakes or misunderstandings before they happen. Acquiring a foreign language perfectly implies mastering the redundancy system; hence the caricature of the Indian in westerns, supposedly incapable of acquiring redundant features, who says in broken English: 'White man speak with forked tongue.'

[4] Quoted in Augarde (1984).

4 The Canny Canner
The Speech Chain and its Components

Word Boundaries

Language seems to divide up quite naturally into words which, for speakers, constitute the basic 'building-blocks' or 'links' of speech. Words, for us speakers, represent the reality of language and learning a language—be it our own or a foreign one—is all about identifying word boundaries. Recognizing these enables us, for example, to distinguish between these two lines of verse:

> Gall, doll-over, ghost to royalty at right hour
> Galled all over, goes to royal tea at Rye Tower

Or again, it enables us to make the right divisions in these trick sentences from children's traditional word games:

> How much wood would a woodchuck chuck
> If a woodchuck could chuck wood?
> As much wood as a woodchuck would chuck
> If a woodchuck could chuck wood
>
> If you can do what a tucan can do
> You two can do what two tucans can do
>
> A canner exceedingly canny
> one morning remarked to his granny:
> 'A canny canner can can
> Anything that he can
> But a canner can't can a can, can he?'

When recognizing the word boundaries we also recognize the fact that in a sequence such as *can a can, can he?*, three different units of meaning correspond to the same word form *can*—an instance of *homophony*. Indeed, identifying the word boundaries goes hand in hand with recognizing the homophony: if word boundaries become blurred, homophony turns into a puzzle, trap or pun: and it is, of course, often used deliberately in this way.

In the written form of the language, word boundaries are made material as gaps—gaps whose absence makes a text quite unreadable. In spoken language however, cutting up the 'speech chain', to use the metaphor introduced by the Swiss linguist Ferdinand de Saussure, is anything but straight-forward.

In certain languages, word boundaries are easily identified by means of phonetic features. In Czech, for example, the stress always falls on the first syllable of a word.[1] Consequently, each stressed syllable signals the begin-ning of a new word. English, as it happens, has no really effective way of signalling the divisions between words. For one thing stress position is vari-able. Moreover, word stress is subordinated to the stress in each breath-group or tone-unit; a reflection of the syntactic and pragmatic organization of utterances rather than of word boundaries (see Chapter 14). Indeed, when delivered quickly, it is not easy to distinguish between the following:

We're happy to have General Drum # right here
We're happy to have General Drumright # here

What is the General's name? *Drum* or *Drumright*? For the difference to be heard, the speaker has to insert a somewhat artificial pause. The same applies if we are to distinguish between *a name/an aim, a loan/alone, a nice bucket/an ice bucket, the grey tape/the great ape, why choose/white shoes, that's tough/that stuff, night-rate/nitrate*, and so on. This is exploited in school-children's riddles such as:

Q: Why is a thought like the sea?
A: Because it's a notion (an ocean)

In French, where the stress always falls on the last syllable of a word, one nevertheless runs into broadly similar problems. *Esther perd ses verres* is equivalent to *Esther persévère*, as far as the stress pattern is concerned and one has to adopt a stilted intonation and make artificial pauses in order to point up the appropriate word boundaries:

Esther # perd # ses # verres (Esther loses her glasses)
Esther # persévère (Esther perseveres)

Similarly, an utterance in French like *J'sais pas*, is a single stress group and may therefore be interpreted by children and by foreigners as a single word. Furthermore, *liaison* and *elision*, both highly characteristic of French, mean that word separation is a hit-and-miss affair, since words literally merge into one another. The elimination of *hiatus*—the juxtaposition of two vowel sounds—and the dropping of final *e* (except, of course, in the speech of the South of France) together make of any French sentence a virtually uninterrupted sequence (80 per cent) of open syllables: an open syllable being one which ends in a vowel, a closed syllable with a consonant. Witness once again children's word games:

---

[1] Cf. Jakobson (1976).

Toutou, ton thé t-a-t-il ôté ta toux?
[tututõtetatilotetatu][2]

A similar liaison phenomenon in English is that of the linking *r*, as in *this beer~is good*. So-called 'intrusive' *r*'s occur in sequences such as *this idear~is good, I sawr~it* and so on.[3]

Children (and foreigners whose only contact with a language is oral) often make false divisions between words because word boundaries are not properly recognized. And it is hardly surprising that such false divisions are very often to be found in words borrowed by one language from another, or in pidgins and creoles. English *an apron*, to take one example, comes, by way of metanalysis or misdivision—misty vision?—from the French *un napperon*. A *nickname* was originally an *eke-name* and *an orange* comes from Spanish *naranja*. Terms which have come into English from Arabic via misdivision often contain the definite article, *al*, as in *alcohol, alcove, algebra*. Malagasy words borrowed from French also incorporate the definite article: as in, *ny latabatra* (from *la table*), *ny larmoara* (from *l'armoire*), *ny lafimetatra* (from *la fenêtre*). Similarly, French-based creoles contain such terms as *nomme* (from *un homme*), *zarbre* (from *les arbres*), *zoizo* (from *les oiseaux*), *zabrico* (from *les abricots*).[4] In the Pidgin English of the Solomon Islands, all verbs are preceded by the prefix, *i-*, derived from the unstressed or 'weak' form of the third-person pronoun *he*, as in: *mifela i-go* (we go), *win i-kom* (the wind comes). Similarly, a prefix *im-*, coming from *him*, is systematically added to all verbs used transitively, as in: *lookoutim fish* (to look out for fish).

Difficulties of word division are exploited in riddles and rhymes whose aim is to educate through play: such creative pieces are clearly designed to make children aware of a source of ambiguity in their language. A child who has just fallen into the trap cannot resist going straight off to try out the new trick on someone else!

Q: Why did the owl 'owl?
A: Because the woodpecker would peck 'er.
Q: Why did the fly fly?
A: Because the spider spied 'er.

After all, what would be the point of all these ambiguities if you could not play with them?

---

[2] See Fig. 6.2 in Ch. 6 for a chart of vowel sounds. The symbol ~ above a vowel (as in õ) indicates a nasalized vowel.

[3] More about post-vocalic [r] in Ch. 6.

[4] This has a very interesting consequence: while very few words have initial /z/ in French, in creoles there is an overwhelming number of them.

The Units of Speech

When Ferdinand de Saussure, the founder of modern linguistics, introduced the metaphor of the 'speech chain', he was suggesting a linking process by analogy with the links in a chain.

Every code is composed of units, signs or symbols which, when joined together, form messages. This is how the musical code works as well as Amerindian systems of smoke signals, or mathematics, cybernetics, and so on. But human language is endowed with a *double* articulation: something which is peculiar to it as compared with other codes and a fact which makes the image of the 'chain' misleading.

Language is structured, on one level, as *units of sound*, and, on a higher level, as *units of meaning* (and we shall see that these do not necessarily correspond to words). There are thus two sorts of links: sounds (devoid of meaning) which serve to form higher level units, which do have meaning and which, in their turn, are linked to form sentences. The units of sound are called *phonemes* and the units of meaning *morphemes*. We shall return to each of these respectively in the next two chapters.

Chain and Choice

Because it is linear, the linguistic message can be projected along an axis which, by convention, is represented as a horizontal line going from left to right—clearly a reflection of the way we write in the West. This means that units of different kinds and different levels are required to follow each other in a certain way in accordance with the rules of co-occurrence specific to each language. This horizontal axis, symbolizing the 'speech chain' is called the *syntagmatic* axis or axis of *combination*.

But dividing this chain—the syntagmatic axis—into words or morphemes, then into syllables and sounds, necessarily implies that each separated segment, once isolated off from the rest of the chain, corresponds to a choice made by the speaker among all the choices s/he could have made. Any message thus presupposes a series or succession of choices, at every point along the utterance, between what is said and what *could* have been said.

Intersecting with the horizontal axis of combination we thus find at each link in the chain a succession of vertical axes of selection. These are called paradigmatic and contain the inventory, for each segment of the utterance, of all those units which can perform the same function in the same context (see Figure 4.1).

To illustrate this, let us turn again to our line of verse, *but a canner can't can a can, can he?*

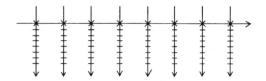

Fɪɢ. 4.1. Vertical axes: lists of possible choices
Horizontal axis: combinatorial constraints

A number of different substitutions can be made in the axis of selection, while retaining the same context. The substitutions can affect a group of words or *phrase*, or only an isolated word. The only requirement is that every unit in each column must be compatible with any unit in the adjacent columns, so as to always form acceptable utterances. Thus, from the following lists:

1	2	3	4
a canner	can [1]	(not) can [2]	a can [3]
this buzzer	could	(not) buy	his sandwich
the freak	should	(not) eat	the starfish
the dinosaur	will	(not) like	our meal
silly Billy	must	(not) wrap	this food

the following sentences, among others, can be formed:

Silly Billy will not eat his sandwich
The dinosaur should not like this food
The freak must not eat the starfish

and so on.

We can see in the resulting sentences that the axis of *combination* presents us with a series of *contrasts* between units of different, yet compatible nature and function. Saussure calls this relationship *in praesentia*: that is, the units making up the message are actually there, present, in their succession. The axis of *selection*, on the other hand, offers a series of *oppositions* (as distinct from contrasts) between mutually exclusive units of the same rank and status. This virtual relationship is termed *in absentia*.

What is most remarkable about our canning example is that a native speaker intuitively knows that he should substitute an auxiliary for *can* [1], a lexical verb for *can* [2], and a noun for *can* [3], without being in the least troubled by the homophony.

This demonstrates the solidarity, or interdependence of *paradigmatic* and *syntagmatic* relationships (i.e. choice and chain relationships).

It is this interdependence which is disregarded in the game of 'cadavre exquis', so dear to the Surrealists (more about this in Chapter 11).

Morphemes and Phonemes

Substitutions can also be made in parts of words: roots, suffixes, prefixes, and endings. And here the game can get rather more complicated since, although the word certainly constitutes the basic unit of meaning for speakers, it is possible to identify units of meaning which are *smaller* than words. The smallest unit which can be separated out from a context while retaining an autonomous meaning, is called a *morpheme*. In the list of forms of the verb *to can* (*can*, *cans*, *canning*, *canned*), we can make a distinction each time between the root and the ending. These constitute two distinct morphemes, because they carry different meanings which may be combined but are independent. The respective status of the word and the morpheme has yet to be clarified: this will be the subject of the next chapter.

Below the level of the morpheme, we might want to consider the *syllable*. But dividing words into syllables is only relevant if each syllable corresponds to a morpheme. In fact, this is often the case in English, where numerous morphemes are monosyllabic. We could note, in passing, that the shortest syllable consists of a vowel. A consonant, by contrast, cannot be articulated in the absence of vocalic support.[5]

At a still lower level, if we take the word can, consisting of three sounds, /k/, /æ/, /n/, we can carry out a number of substitutions for each sound[6]:

can /kæn/	can /kæn/	can /kæn/
ban /bæn/	kin /kɪn/	cat /kæt/
pan /pæn/	keen /kiːn/	cap /kæp/
fan /fæn/	corn /kɔːn/	cab /kæb/
tan /tæn/	cane /keɪn/	cash /kæʃ/

and so on. Note that a different word is obtained each time by changing one sound only, while the rest of the phonic context remains the same. Each language has its own inventory of *distinctive* consonant and vowel sounds, which linguists call *phonemes*. I deal with the phoneme in Chapter 6.

Further divisions are not possible, although, as we shall see in Chapter 6, phonemes can themselves be broken down into distinctive *features*, which are substitutable.

So, we can now appreciate that segmentation and substitution operate at different levels, underlining the existence of units of different rank. From the

[5] In those languages which appear to have syllables composed of consonants—such as Czech or Serbo-Croat—so-called 'neutral' vowels are in fact inserted.

[6] The unfamiliar vowel symbols come from the International Phonetic Alphabet or IPA. See Figs. 6.1 and 6.3 in Ch. 6 for a full discussion of the vowels in English, and Fig. 6.5 for the consonants in English.

phoneme to the sentence—the upper limit[7]—these different levels are organized into a hierarchy. This hierarchy appears clearly if we try to break down a sentence into its constituents (see Figure 4.2).

phoneme	ə/ k/æ/n/i/ k/æ/n/ə/ k/ə/n/ k/æ/n/
morpheme	a can-ny can-ner can can any-thing
word	a canny canner can can anything
phrase	[a canny canner] [can can anything]
	noun phrase *verb phrase*
clause	[A canny canner can can anything] [that he can]
	main clause *subordinate clause*
sentence	A canny canner can can anything that he can

FIG. 4.2. The hierarchy of units

A language can be analysed in a number of different ways. Segmentation and substitution form the basis of *distributional analysis*, which is certainly the first step towards *describing* the structure of a language, even though it provides no *explanation* of this structure.

Distributional analysis is precisely what we need in order to distinguish between homophones from different word classes or with different functions: we might carry out a search for a list of units compatible with a common context, and conversely the search for all possible contexts in which a given unit might appear. As we have just seen in *the canner can't can a can*, the same sound sequence repeated three times is interpreted without difficulty as *auxiliary, verb, noun* (in the context, obviously, of the whole sentence) because the three forms are defined by different word class contexts. So much so that homophony (except in the case of blurred word boundaries) poses no real threat to communication when the homophones are from different classes. This is fortunate, since numerous monosyllables in English are affected by homophony—*I can't bear to see a bare bear; that's not the way to weigh the whey*. This is distinct from *homography*—which concerns pairs of words written in an identical way, but which may be pronounced differently (to r*e*ad v. he r*e*ad)—and from *polysemy* (see Chapter 13).

At whatever level we apply them, therefore, selection and combination represent the two basic organizing principles of language. Indeed, a deficiency in one or the other of these mechanisms is responsible for two major types of aphasia, one manifesting itself by an inability to organize syntagmatic relationships, the other by an inability to substitute one word with another, or with a periphrasis, a definition, a synonym, antonym, generic term or even a unit having the same function.[8]

[7] Of course sentences are themselves components of bigger stretches of speech, linked by various cohesive devices, but here we are not dealing with units of the same kind: sentences cannot be organized in paradigms. We do not form texts by selecting ready-made sentences.

[8] Cf. Jakobson (1941).

5 Anti-dis-establish-ment-arian-ism
Words and Morphemes

'In a word', 'in other words', 'to eat one's words', 'don't mince your words', 'you took the words right out of my mouth': all these idioms—and many others—bear witness to the fact that, where speakers are concerned, the formal unit of language is clearly the *word*: a mobile, autonomous unit.

A first useful distinction can be drawn between *content* (or *lexical*) words and *structure* (or *function*) words. Words in the first group—nouns, adjectives, verbs, adverbs—can form complete utterances on their own: 'Tomorrow!', 'Lovely!', 'Jump!', 'When?'. Those in the second group, however—articles, conjunctions, prepositions, particles—can never appear alone.

The Architecture of Words

The existence of words seems intuitively obvious to speakers. Are we then to believe that the *morpheme* is a mere invention of linguists? Since it sometimes corresponds to a word, but more often than not to a part of a word, the morpheme lacks the clear autonomy which characterizes the word and is not so easily identified. In a way, its definition is a negative one: it is 'the smallest unit of meaning' beyond which no further division can be made while still retaining some autonomous meaning.

And yet, if we didn't realize how morphemes are articulated, if we were not aware of the 'architecture' of words, we could learn neither how to conjugate verbs, nor—in those languages where the problem arises—how to decline nouns, nor interpret new words formed from new combinations of existing morphemes (*phonology*, for example, can be interpreted as 'the science of sounds' by one who knows the meaning of *phono*graph and bio*logy*): nor could we create new words, of course, by the process known as *neologism* which consists, precisely, of drawing anew on existing elements.

Identifying morphemes, however, is no easy task. Let us return to an example from the previous chapter:

A canny canner can can
Anything that he can,
But a canner can't can a can, can he?

If we change the last line into a positive statement (leaving the patent absurdity of the sentence to one side!), we can then derive the following transformations from it:

(1) the canner cans cans
(2) the canner is canning a can
(3) the canner has canned a can
(4) the canner canned a can
(5) the canner will can the can
(6) the canner cans cans, boxes and crates
(7) the canner's canning of the can can be uncanny

We can oppose the first occurence of *cans* in (1) to *is canning* in (2). As we saw in the previous chapter they belong to the same *paradigmatic axis*. The root morpheme, *can*, is the same, so the variation allows us to distinguish between the idea of a habitual action and the idea of an action in progress. But how do we account for the fact that, in one case, the verb consists of two words, while it is one word in the other case? We can solve the problem—and here morphology demonstrates its ability to operate at a certain level of abstraction—by calling the auxiliary *be*, in association with *-ing* (the mark of the present participle) a *discontinuous* morpheme, with the meaning {incomplete aspect} (of the action). Thanks to this sleight of hand, *is . . . ing* acquires the same status—in respect of the root *can*—as the ending *-s*. This is also what happens in (3), for the combination *has . . . ed*, with the meaning of {completed action} and in (5) where the combination of modal auxiliary *will* + bare infinitive is to be interpreted as {future tense}. Discontinuous morphemes are predominant in the verb system of modern English (including the expression of tense, aspect, and modality); it is very much an *analytic* system.

But English also contains *synthetic* morphemes. In (1), as in (2) and (3), the same morpheme *-s* appears, simultaneously bearing three different meanings: {present tense}, {third person}, and {singular}—quite a lot of work for such a small morpheme to do. Because it cannot be broken down, we shall dub it a 'portmanteau' morpheme.

In contrast to what happens in other Indo-European languages, English verbs do not use specific morphemes to mark the 'persons' other than third singular. The {third-person singular/present tense} morpheme *-s*, therefore, stands in paradigmatic opposition at every other point in the conjugation with a *meaningful absence*, for which we have to make room in our system of oppositions: and here we speak of a *zero* morpheme. This constitutes, therefore, a unit of meaning in the fullest sense and requires us to recognize the existence of an abstract form, quite unsupported by any concrete realization. In contrast to the {third-person singular/present tense} *-s*, the *-ed* in (4) only assumes the meaning of {past tense}, since it appears as standard in all persons (with the exception of the verb *to be*).

Many *grammatical* morphemes—since this is what we are discussing—exhibit homonymy: thus *-ed* appears in (3) and in (4) as *two* different morphemes—{past participle} or {simple past}. This is also true of *-ing* in (2) and (7), where the first occurrence is read as a verb ending and the second as a noun suffix. Lastly, *-s* appears in (6) and (7) as *three* different morphemes: {plural of a noun}, {third-person singular/present tense}, and {genitive case}.

We can use the first of these values {plural of a noun} to illustrate another aspect of morphology's capacity for abstraction. In (6), the {plural} morpheme *-s*, written identically in each case, is realized in speech in three different ways:

/kænz/ /kreits/ /bɒksɪz/

The rule is simple: *-s* is realized as /s/ after a voiceless consonant, /z/ after a voiced consonant or a vowel, and /ɪz/ after a sibilant.[1] The variation—which affects the morpheme *-s*—whichever of the values in (6) and (7) are concerned—is manipulated quite unconsciously by the speaker, who automatically produces the required form according to the phonetic context. What we are talking about here are combinatorial or contextual variants, called *allomorphs*. Each of the three homonymic morphemes *-s*, consequently, possesses the same allomorphs.

And so we see that, compared with the word—a concrete, easy to grasp unit—the morpheme seems relatively abstract. It is, indeed, the product of analysis.

Finally, we need to point out that among grammatical morphemes, some are bound (*inflectional* morphemes such as *-s*, *-ed*, *-ing* . . . exemplified above). Others are *free* (*a*, *the*, *of*, *that* . . .) and coincide with words.

The same distinction can be made where *lexical* morphemes are concerned. They are said to be free when they correspond to a word. In present-day English, the native lexical stock (of Germanic origin) includes a large number of one-morpheme words. Lexical morphemes are said to be *bound*, however, when they can appear only in compact combinations: this is the case with all morphemes derived from ancient Greek (*phono-*, *morpho-* etc., referred to as *paleo-morphemes*) and with all derivational morphemes (suffixes, prefixes, etc.) which contribute to the formation of complex words: in English, this often means *Latinate* words. The two oppositions—free/bound and grammatical/lexical—form a criss-cross pattern. The first rests on a formal criterion, the second on a criterion of meaning.

---

[1] For a definition of these phonetic terms see Ch. 6. Sibilants are a subset of the fricative consonants

Language Change and Lexical Innovation

TEACHER. Let us continue. I said, 'Let us continue'. Take the word *front*. Well, have you?
PUPIL. Yes, yes. I have. Oh, my teeth, my teeth.
TEACHER. The word *front* is the root in *frontispiece*. As it is in *effrontery*. -*ispiece* is a suffix and *ef*- is a prefix. They are so called because they do not change. They do not want to.

Unfortunately, things are not always quite as straightforward as Eugene Ionesco makes them seem in this extract from *The Lesson*. Phonetic evolution and irregularities can combine to make breaking words down into their component parts a hit-or-miss affair. A child needs considerable capacity for abstraction in order to identify the same kind of relationship between *be* and *was*, as between *love* and *loved*, or to identify in *reception*, the same root as in *receive* and then to discover that they are linked in the same way as *working* and *work*. Moreover, an analysis which is valid from a *historical* or *etymological* point of view may be worthless from the *synchronic* point of view: that is, within the language system as it exists and is perceived by speakers at a given moment in its history. We would be deceiving ourselves if we believed that all speakers perceive language in the same way. There is necessarily a difference between those who know how to write and those who do not (children and the non-illiterate) insofar as the history of the language can be read in its spelling. The speakers' level of education is also a factor. For European languages this includes their knowledge of Greek or Latin roots and of the origin of borrowed words. It is not at all easy, if one is not a specialist, to relate *bishop* to *episcopal*, *chief* to *capital*, *channel* to *canal*, or *heart* to *cardiac*, even though these pairs of words are linked both by their etymology and by their current meaning.

Sometimes, the complete form of Latin words has come down to us, but not their constituent morphemes. If we compare *amplitude* and *turpitude*, for example, we can easily isolate the suffix -*itude*, which we also find in numerous abstract nouns and which is still productive—that is, it is a morpheme which may still be used to create new words, although not with native stems. But, in the first case, *ampl*- is identified as a morpheme of English, found in *ample*, *amply*, *amplify*, and so on, while *turp*- is not: an accident of history has meant that in one case the adjective and words derived from it have all passed into English, while in the other case they have not. So the independence of the morpheme *turp*- can only rest on a knowledge of the Latin *turpis*. A similar case would be the suffix -*age*, which combines in a number of loan words with morphemes which are unidentifiable in English—as in, **bever**-*age*, **carn**-*age*, **foli**-*age*—whereas segmentation is obvious in **carri**-*age*, **marri**-*age*, **pilgrim**-*age*. This is the problem with so-called *paleo-morphemes*, whose status and meaning are impenetrable for many speakers. Such morphemes are all the more numerous in English, insofar as it is a hybrid language which has borrowed a great deal, in particular from the classical and Romance languages.

This opacity of morphemes gives rise to folk etymology, which distinguishes false morphemes. Folk etymologists liken foreign morphemes to morphemes in the mother tongue. Thus, *pantry*, from the French *panetière*, 'bread basket', is reinterpreted by English speakers as 'a place to store *pans*', *sandals* as 'shoes to walk in the *sand*', *asparagus* is deformed as *sparrow-grass*, and *varicose veins* as *very close veins*. The same phenomenon of false etymology has, in French, allowed the creation of **mono**kini to refer to a topless bathing suit, from **bi**kini (derived by metonymy from the name of a Pacific atoll, but perceived as containing the morpheme **bi**).

More surprisingly, a foreign derivational morpheme may become productive in the borrower language. In this way, when the Soviets sent the first *sputnik* into space in the 1950s, the suffix *-nik* was picked up by young Americans and became very productive in the counter-culture, yielding **beatnik, peacenik, lovenik**, etc.

Finally, the meaning of a morpheme can be redefined through metonymy and begin a new career. Following Watergate, *-gate* was given a new meaning, namely 'criminal scandal involving politicians', whence came *Contragate* and *Irangate*. In the 1990s, this new craze crossed the Atlantic—in the time-honoured fashion—and produced *Camillagate* and even *Sharongate* (for the aficionados of one successful British soap opera).

Analogy and Over-Regularization

> Forth from his den to steal he stole,
> His bags of chink he chunk,
> And many a wicked smile he smole,
> And many a wink he wunk.

goes the nursery rhyme

Children gradually acquire the notion of a variable morpheme by a process of trial and error, which brings them, at first, to work by analogy, based on combinations of regular morphemes. The child's analogical remodelling, or over-regularization, is corrected by the adults around it. In due course, the child will learn to say *I bit*, not *I bote*, *I brought* not *I bringed* or *I brang*, *feet* and not *foots*. When it concerns the entire community, however, over-regularization is a motor of language evolution. In this way, the morpheme for the plural of nouns, *-s*, characteristic of one class of nouns in Old English (namely, the 'stone' class), was extended by analogy to *all* nouns, thus eliminating the other marks of plurality, with the exception of all but a small number of words, such as *mouse* and *man* (note however, that in modern usage the plural of a computer *mouse* is *mouses* and the plural of *Walkman* is *Walkmans*).There can also be variation between dialects as in *I dove* (US) vs. *I dived* (British).

> The plural of tooth is teeth;
> Is the plural of booth then beeth?
> The plural of mouse is mice;
> Is the plural of spouse then spice?
> The plural of that is those;
> Is the plural of hat then hose,
> And the plural of rat then rose?
> Who knows?

Uglification: Morphological Gaps and Virtual Words

The vocabulary or lexis of a language is very much an open-ended list. Drawing on the stock of available morphemes and, given the rules for possible morphonological combinations in each language, one can construct all the words one likes and ascribe meanings to them. There is thus an infinite number of *virtual* words just waiting to appear and to cover new concepts, plug gaps, re-establish symmetries. There even exists a computer program tirelessly forming combinations of the morphemes of the English language and ascribing a plausible definition to each new word obtained.

And yet, dissymmetries abound in all languages. The existing morpheme combinations are riddled with holes. Possible and useful words have quite forgotten to come into existence. There are incomplete series of words and negative terms which have no corresponding positive term. Thus, while French has the adjective *chevelu* (implying a mop of hair) and English has *disshevelled* (scruffy, untidy hair and general appearance), French has no **déchevelu* and English lacks **shevelled*. Other dissymmetrical pairs in English are *uncouth/*couth*, *mischievous/*chievous*, *distraught/*traught*, *mishap/*hap*, *distress/*tress*, *disgusting/*gusting*, *disgruntled/*gruntled*. Verbs have forgotten to produce nouns, or the reverse. A number of nouns for male agency—professor, supervisor, etc.—have no female equivalent: **professoress*, **supervisoress*, **doctoress*, **directoress*, and many others are virtual words.[2]

None of this, of course, prevents speakers from playing with these unrealized words: as in, 'I do like George, don't you? So couth!', said by one customer in a London public house about another who had just left; or 'the gruntling of middle England', in a British Sunday paper on government attempts to woo back its traditional electorate. Not to mention Lewis

---

[2]   Cf. R. Lakoff (1975) for English and Yaguello (1978) and (1989) for French.

Carroll's creations, of course. While French has a verb *embellir* which is opposed to *enlaidir*, English only has to *beautify*, a fact which gives Carroll's Gryphon a pretext, when he meets Alice, in Wonderland, for inventing to *uglify*, a perfectly acceptable potential word. Humpty Dumpty, in a similar fashion, opposes *birthday present* and *unbirthday present*.

Neologism

Neologism, the creation of new words, actualizes the morphological composition of a word, make it plain to see for everyone at the synchronic level, before history has time to blur the outlines. 'Neologism', to quote Jakobson, 'forces us to think etymologically.'

Neologism flourishes most where official academic bodies cannot repress it, that is in slang and in colloquial or popular speech: but also in scientific and technical language—somewhat paradoxically, since that register might be labelled as the most 'academic' of all (in the literal sense of that term). It is indeed the inalienable right of academics and researchers to create their own terminology. In this way, computer wizards have coined, for example, *software* (by analogy with *hardware*), followed by *firmware, manware, shareware, freeware*, and even the more politically correct *peopleware*, not to mention to *debug*, to *download*, and dozens more. And of course linguists coin new words as fast as they come up with new concepts.

Neologism is often an economical way of responding to the specific, sometimes ephemeral needs of communication. Among examples found in the press are *mediarology*—'the didactic use of the media to alert the general public to the consequences of global warming';[3] *hazardologist*—'expert in the hazards of life';[4] *gastronaut*—'astronaut with gastronomic tastes'.[5] We should delight in this phenomenon, rather than bemoan it, since it proves the dynamism of any language and the sense of humour of its speakers, far preferable (in my opinion) to lazy borrowing from another language.

Portmanteau words, such as *gastronaut*, are a special type of neologism. Related to the slip of the tongue, to the pun and to lexical creativity proper, they show an amalgam of two words having a segment in common, though the latter is not necessarily a morpheme (a unit of meaning). Common examples are *smog* (*smoke* + *fog*) characteristic of post-war London and *motel* (*motor* + *hotel*) which originated in the United States or again *motorcade* from *cavalcade* and *ambucopter* from *helicopter*. *Butskellism* (from Butler and Gaitskell, Labour and Conservative Chancellors, respectively) neatly encapsulated the consensual approach to economic policy in post-war Britain, *stagflation* summed up an unusual and uncomfortable economic reality in

---

[3] *Scientific American*, 2 Nov. 1989.   [4] *Telegraph Sunday Magazine*, 11 Dec. 1988.
[5] *Newsweek*, 1 Feb. 1988. All these examples are from GRIL (1993).

the 1970s, while *cocacolonization* conjures up the image of American economic imperialism. *Morphonology* and *onomatopoetics* are linguists' portmanteau words. *Workaholic* is a striking short-cut for defining someone who works to an excessive degree, as *shopaholic* is for one gripped by a purchasing frenzy, or *chocaholic* for one in the grip of the demon cocoa. Similarly, *Afristocracy* indicts the new South African elites, while *edutainment* or *infotainment* designates the CD-ROM industry. The development of the Internet has very rapidly led to the creation of a specific etiquette called *netiquette* and the tunnel under the Channel could not fail to be called the *Chunnel*.

The unintentional portmanteau word is related to the slip of the tongue or mispronunciation (see below Chapter 10). Lewis Carroll, Edward Lear, or more recently John Lennon, have practised it as a form of amusing or poetic invention. The famous poem *Jabberwocky*, a central element in *Through the Looking Glass* and which we shall be considering later, is crammed with such terms. Some of the portmanteau terms invented by Carroll (for example, *galumph*) have even entered the hallowed pages of the *Oxford English Dictionary*.

Portmanteau words can be expressive, witty, or poetic. Not so the words composed of truncated syllables, so characteristic of Soviet Russia or Nazi Germany, as for example *komsomol* (a youth organization in Soviet Russia) or *kolkhoze* (a collective farm) or the sinister war-time *Gestapo*: these are purely practical creations which have achieved complete lexicalization. They seem to be particularly popular in totalitarian regimes. This is the reason why George Orwell used just this feature to characterize Newspeak, the language spoken in his novel *1984*: in the land of 'Big Brother' the police forces include a *thinkpol* (thought police), a *pornsec* (pornography section), a *ficdep* (fiction department), and so on.

Acronyms, composed of the initial letters and not sections of words, are easily lexicalized to the extent that they lend themselves to easy pronunciation and are adapted to the morphology of the language: *radar* (radio detecting and ranging) or *aids* (acquired immune deficiency syndrome) are cases in point. Users are no longer aware of the components. This type of word formation—often humorous- is very much in fashion, as in *yuppy* ('young urban professional') or, more recently, *zippy* ('zen-inspired pronoia professional'), *nimby* ('not in my back yard') or *dinky* ('dual income no kids').

In order to become legitimate members of the lexicon, neologisms must be sanctioned by the authority of the dictionary or by official use. And yet all speakers coin words in everyday usage, in earnest or in jest: a fact which brings us to the very interesting question of individual creativity within language—a collective phenomenon. Why do some word creations catch on within the linguistic community while others do not? Fashion trends are certainly at work here. Speakers eagerly pick up new words, following the lead of some dynamic innovator within their social group, but are sometimes just as prompt to discard them.

In this way new words keep cropping up while old ones disappear from usage. While the grammar of a language changes very slowly its lexicon is in a state of constant flux.

Grammaticization

Lexical morphemes and content words belong to so-called *open* classes: new ones are created all the time as we have seen and there is no limit to the vocabulary of any language. Grammatical morphemes and function words on the other hand are members of *closed* classes; these classes resist innovation and are fairly stable; new grammatical morphemes however do develop over time via the process of *grammaticization*, while others disappear. But the process is much slower and speakers are not generally aware of it.

How are new function words or grammatical morphemes created? Across languages, linguists have noticed that these derive from 'frozen' uses of lexical morphemes. For instance, prepositions are very often based on names of body parts, as in Wolof:

kanam	'face'	ci kanamu X	'in front of X'
biir	'belly'	ci biiru X	'inside X'
wet	'flank', 'side'	ci wetu X	'beside X'
ginnnaaw	'back'	ci ginnaaw(u) X	'behind X'
ndigg	'waist'	ci diggante X ak Y	'between X and Y'

and so on.

In English complex prepositions we can also identify lexical morphemes denoting body parts: in *front* of, be*hind*, a*head* of, at the *foot* of, in the *back* of, be*side*, out*side*, be*fore*, etc.

English auxiliaries (*do*, *have*, *shall*, *will*, etc.) are grammaticized lexical verbs. French has developed a series of aspectual auxiliaries from verbs meaning 'to begin', 'to stop', to continue', 'to be in the process of', 'to fail', etc.

Articles are often derived from numerals as the English indefinite article with its three allomorphs *a*, *an*, *one*.

Interestingly, these changes may be cyclical. English has come all the way from synthetic to analytic. What is the next cycle going to be?

6 Did You Say Pig or Fig?
The Sound Systems of Languages

'Take away his rants and the poor baron has nothing. What a difference a vowel makes!—If his *rents* were but equal to his *rants*!'

(Jane Austen, *Mansfield Park*)

'Did you say pig or fig?' says the Cheshire Cat to Alice. This is a typically metalinguistic question. Whenever we mishear what is said, as users of language we put our finger, or rather we put our *ear*, on the fact that a single sound is enough to change the meaning of an otherwise identical sound sequence.

The converse of a misunderstanding, on the speaker's side, is the 'slip of the tongue'. The speaker may mistakenly transpose two sounds, either within a phrase (*our queer dean* for *our dear queen*) or over a whole sentence. The former case is an example of the classic 'spoonerism', so named after the Reverend W. A. Spooner (1844–1930), an Oxford don who is famous for saying 'I have never addressed so many tons of soil' at a workers' meeting; or who, when telling off a student, is supposed to have said 'You have hissed all my mystery lectures. You will leave by the next town drain.' It is well known that these slips of the tongue occupy an important place in Freudian theory. It is perhaps less obvious that they should also hold a special interest for linguists. In fact, misunderstandings, slips of the tongue, as well as the deliberate exploitation of paronymy (words which are almost identical) to create rhyme, whether in poetry, children's riddles and nonsense verse, or advertising: all of these highlight the *distinctive* function of phonemes (first pointed out in Chapter 4). Or, to be more precise, such accidents of speech highlight the importance of that function and, at the same time, point to its extreme vulnerability. For, if the phoneme as a unit of sound is itself devoid of meaning, its role is nonetheless to *establish* the meaning of higher level units: the meaning of the morpheme or of the word, or that of a whole sequence of words when these constitute a breath-group. The phoneme, in a sense, is the weak link in the language chain, or, mixing our metaphors, the door through which changes can most easily enter the language.

Speech and Writing: Phonemes vs. Letters

However obvious it may seem, I must emphasize here that phonemes are units of the *spoken* language and not the *written* language. Writing is an attempt to represent the spoken language graphically, an attempt which, for all sorts of reasons, often falls short of the spoken reality and is therefore misleading: all the more so since terms such as *vowel* and *consonant* are used to describe both the written code and the oral code. Consequently, a speaker of English grows up, from infant school onwards, under the illusion that the language has just five vowels, ⟨a⟩ ⟨e⟩ ⟨i⟩ ⟨o⟩ ⟨u⟩, when in fact these are the *written* vowel symbols. Few speakers are aware that standard British English includes twelve vowel phonemes and eight diphthongs: a thoroughly respectable total of twenty distinctive vocalic sounds (see Figure 6.1). Moreover, the total varies slightly across dialects. Indeed, between languages which share the same writing system, there can be large variations in the numbers of vowel phonemes. Thus, standard French has thirteen, while Italian has seven.

The difficulty here stems from the fact that in cultures with a long written tradition, we are so conditioned to think in terms of the alphabet and to divide words into *letters* that we are more often than not deaf, as it were, to what we hear. This explains why most people are able to say at once how many letters there are in a given word (especially crossword enthusiasts!), yet have difficulty in establishing the number of phonemes in the same word. Since spoken language is acquired naturally, through contact with the people around us, while the written language demands, by contrast, a long and difficult learning process, it is perhaps understandable that speakers tend to reserve their powers of analysis for the written language and take the spoken language for granted. A simple, but revealing test serves to illustrate the point. Ask those around you to think of words ending in ⟨u⟩. They will answer something like: 'Let's see, apart from *you* and *flu* (which is an abbreviation anyway) I can't think of any.' And, true enough, the *letter* ⟨u⟩ hardly ever appears at the end of a word. And yet, final /juː/ is actually very frequent in English, as shown by such common words as *few*, *due*, *hue*, etc. It is only inside a word that the sound group [juː] can be *written* ⟨u⟩, as in pupil /pjuːpl/.

Now do the same test with the letter ⟨e⟩. Of course, this is much easier. Lots of English words end in ⟨e⟩ . . . But *do* they? The ⟨e⟩, more often than not, is silent. According to an English spelling convention, the role of the final ⟨e⟩ after a consonant is to show that the preceding vowel is either long or a diphthong. Oppositions such as the following are created in this way: *met/mete, mat/mate, mad/made, bad/bade, not/note, bit/bite,* and so on. But this convention itself derives from the fact that English suffers from a shortage of *written* vowel symbols. When we come to French, the situation, to be frank, is almost perverse: words written with a final ⟨e⟩ are pronounced with a final consonant, whereas words which end with a written consonant actually end in a vowel when they are spoken, because the majority of final consonants are silent!

Literate speakers therefore have a completely distorted image of their own language, since the written form is engraved in their minds and interferes with phonemic reality. This we fail to see even though it is staring us in the face: or perhaps we should rather say, this we fail to hear, even though it is bellowing at us.

The Spelling System

The languages which have the longest written tradition are also those where we find the most striking differences between sounds and the way these are written down. However, the attitude of linguistic communities towards spelling as a social norm is variable. Not all nations, that is, are as conservative as Britain or France in this area. Spain, Norway, Russia, and Italy, to quote only a few examples, have proved willing to adapt their writing system to take account of the realities of sound change.

The alphabet inherited from Latin, though perfectly adequate for that language, has never been appropriate for the European languages which adopted it and for which it has never really been more than a makeshift solution. The unsuitability was compounded, paradoxically, by mutual borrowings beween languages, and by the creation of terms from Latin roots: so much so, in fact, that a completely arbitrary principle now appears to reign supreme within the spelling system of English, as illustrated by the following anonymous poem:

> When the English tongue we speak
> Why is break not rhymed with freak?
> Will you tell me why it's true
> We say sew but likewise few?
> And the maker of this verse
> Cannot rhyme his horse with worse.
> Beard sounds not the same as heard;
> Cord is different from word;
> Shoe is never rhymed with foe.
> Think of hose and dose and lose,
> And of goose and choose:
> Think of comb and tomb and bomb,
> Doll and roll and home and some:
> And since pay is rhymed with say,
> Why not paid with said I pray?

> We have blood and food and good,
> Mould is not pronounced like could.
> How come done, but gone and lone?
> Is there any reason known?
> So, in short, it seems to me,
> Me and English don't agree!!!!!!

Bernard Shaw, who campaigned vigorously for a reform of the English spelling system, even went so far as to quip that a word like *fish* might just as well be written *ghoti*, on the grounds that GH is the same as /f/ in *enough*, O is read as /ɪ/ in *women* and TI is pronounced as a palatal consonant /ʃ/ when it is part of the suffix -*tion*. Shaw, of course, was exaggerating for comic effect. GH is never pronounced like /f/ in initial position. The O of *women* is an exception which cannot be generalized. As for -TI-, its pronunciation is wholly dependent on the context, namely the nominal suffix -*ion* as added to the stem ending in -*t*: *intersect/intersection*. This is entirely predictable, and confined entirely to this context.

But despite all appearances to the contrary, the English writing system is not wholly inconsistent: native speakers generally know how to pronounce new words when they come across them and must therefore have internalized some sort of rule about which sounds correspond to which letter sequences. The most recent work in generative—i.e. Chomskian—phonology, tends to show that in most cases spelling does constitute an accurate reflection of the sound structure of the language. About 80 per cent of English spelling appears to be rule-governed. Irregular spellings such as *women* can usually be explained if not predicted. Loan words may cause problems but neologisms are always regular.

Allowing for inconsistencies, learning how to spell means acquiring knowledge which is not entirely devoid of interest, whatever the most radical proponents of spelling reform would have us believe and even if one can sometimes regret the consequent waste of time and energy at school.[1] For our spelling system, in fact, is a sort of language museum, pitching us way back into the history of the language and its multiple roots: Greek, Latin, Anglo-Saxon, French . . . In its present-day form, the spelling system structures the way we relate to written language, indeed, structures our entire relationship with language, insofar as it forces us to insert divisions, to make

---

[1] Obviously, languages which have developed their writing system during the modern period, based on a more scientific approach, have a considerable advantage (as in the case of many languages of black Africa, the Amerindian languages and most of the languages of the former USSR, etc.), although, in some instances, it is a case of science giving way to ideology: in the USSR, languages transcribed in Latin-based IPA (the International Phonetic Alphabet) during the 1920s, were retranscribed after 1930 in the Cyrillic alphabet in order to facilitate the teaching of Russian and the integration of Russian loan-words. In the French West Indies, the transcription of the creole there still owes too much to 'historical' French.

clear the boundaries which the spoken language leaves unclear and to make perceptible the essentially discrete nature of the word. This is brought home when we read phonetic transcriptions (whether by linguists or humorists or novelists), which are off-putting and slow down our reading, since they smother the familiar patterns of written words. As Mrs Higgins says to her son: 'Though I like to get pretty postcards in your patent shorthand [i.e. phonetic writing], I always have to read the copies in ordinary writing you so thoughtfully send me.'[2]

From all of this, it follows that peoples equipped with a writing system will necessarily have a different perception of language, of its nature and its form, from those peoples who speak unwritten languages. In the same way, people who can read and write do not perceive language in the same way as the non-literate (see the instances, in Chapter 4, of 'false divisions', which characterize the language of young children).

The written word also serves as a link between all the dialects (in the sense of regional and social variants) of a particular language. There are, for example, hundreds of different pronunciations of English, between which mutual comprehension is not necessarily a foregone conclusion. But there is only one spelling (if one leaves aside the comparatively small number of American innovations, such as *lite*, *nite*, or *color*).

When Bernard Shaw transcribes Eliza's Cockney accent in the opening scene of *Pygmalion*: 'Ow, eez yǝ-ooa san, is e? Wal, fewd dan y' dǝ-ooty bawmz a mather should, eed now bettern to spawl a pore gel's flahrzn than ran awy athaht pyin, Will ye-oo py me f' them?' the reader is grateful that he doesn't keep it up in the rest of the play, as it would make it most tiresome to read.

The unifying role of spelling is true of all widely spoken languages. One important consequence of this, in the case of such languages, is that any reform which tried to go in the direction of a phonetic spelling would pose the problem of the choice of a norm, a choice which would inevitably work to the advantage of culturally dominant groups. Indeed, this is one of the major brakes on any far-reaching spelling reform. As noted by George Orwell:

You can only rationalize spelling if you give a fixed value to each letter. But this means standardizing pronunciation, which could not be done in this country without an unholy row. What do you do, for instance, about words like 'butter' or 'glass', which are pronounced in different ways in London and Newcastle? Other words such as 'were' are pronounced in two different ways according to individual inclination, or according to context.[3]

But the spelling system has other advantages, too. Many instances of homophony are resolved by transcriptions which, however absurd they may

---

[2] *Pygmalion*, Act III.   [3] *Tribune*, 14 Mar. 1947. Quoted by Lilly and Viel (1993).

sometimes seem, at least have the merit, in most cases, of being different when the homophones in question have distinct etymologies. And we are, indeed, in the course of everyday life, often required to spell a word in order to remove an ambiguity: 'Do you mean "well-HEALED" or "well-HEELED"?'

From A to Z: The Tradition of Literary Games

The written code, by moving away from the oral code, has in our societies virtually come to be autonomous, and this process has given rise to an important tradition of literary games, which are quite distinct from games based on the phoneme. In many games, letters, as it were, have the starring role and use the alphabet as a carefully ordered structure, with little regard for the sounds involved.

Primer writing, for example, consists of writing a text in which each paragraph, each verse, each line, or each word begins with a different letter, in alphabetical order:

A Born Coward, Darius Eventually Found Great Happiness In Judicially Kicking Loud-Mouthed Nepotists Openly Picking Quarrels, Rightly Saying That Unkindness Vitiated Warring Xerxes Youthful Zeal.

Graham Rawle's **LOST CONSONANTS 7**

HAZELNUT WHIRL FOR PRESIDENT

(203) Gran would spend ages trying to elect a chocolate

The *lipogram* is based on the systematic omission of one of the letters of the alphabet. If the letter in question is ⟨e⟩, then there is something of an air of 'mission impossible' about it. In fact, in the case of English, this amounts to excluding most of the pronouns and the definite article, as well as preventing use of the simple past tense. The American Ernest Vincent Wright, has produced one of these: *Gadsby, A story of over 50 000 words without using the letter E*; and so has the French novelist, Georges Perec, with *La Disparition*.[4] The opposite of the lipogram is the *univocalic*. In both cases, we are dealing with forms of literary affectation.

The *anacyclic* consists of looking for words which can be read equally well from left to right and from right to left, but with a different meaning, as with the Latin ROMA–AMOR. What we have, then, is a 'mirror' reading of the kind which Lewis Carroll exploits in *Sylvie and Bruno Concluded*:

Sylvie was arranging some letters on a board E-V-I-L. 'Now, Bruno', she said, 'what does that spell?' . . . 'Why, it's LIVE, backwards', he exclaimed . . . '.

The *palindrome* has the same meaning whichever direction one reads in:

First find a word that doth silence proclaim
And backwards and forwards is always the same

goes the riddle. Answer: 'MUM's the word!' Or, again:

Madam I'm Adam.
I moan, Naomi.
Live not on evil.
Sex at noon taxes.

Anagrams provide pseudonyms, nicknames, as well as cryptic or amusing ways of referring to people. Salvador Dali was nicknamed *Avida Dollars* and Margaret Thatcher, *That great charmer*, or *Meg, the arch Tartar*. The name *Clint Eastwood* can be rearranged to make *Old West action*; *Victoria, England's Queen* makes *Governs a nice quiet land*, and *William Shakespeare* gives *A weakish speller, am I?* The word *marriage* can be a *grim era*, *funeral* turns into *real fun*, and *revolution* becomes *to love ruin*.[5]

Crosswords, squarewords, Scrabble, Boggle, and other such acrostics belong to the same area. Lewis Carroll was very fond of a little game called 'Doublets', very popular during the Victorian period, which consisted of making a chain of words of equal length, changing one letter each time, so that by starting from a source word one arrives at the designated target word in as few steps as possible. For example:

love to *hate*
love ⟩ live ⟩ hive ⟩ have ⟩ hate

---

[4] Translated into English as *A Void*, by Gilbert Adair.
[5] Many more examples can be found in Augarde (1984).

There are, as we can see, countless games (with new ones constantly being dreamed up) where the basic units are *letters*. Since letters are the (more or less faithful) equivalent of phonemes—the sound units of language—it might seem surprising that letters inspire so many games while phonemes inspire so few. As I have already pointed out, this has a lot to do with cultural tradition. A large number of games based on sound can be found both in societies with an oral tradition and in the games of schoolchildren.

Playing with Sound

Puns, riddles, the spoonerism, and the rebus, play exclusively on the oral language. Of this group, only the spoonerism is based solely on the phoneme.

In actual fact, most letter-based games could quite easily have a phonemic counterpart, provided speakers could be trained to recognize phonemes in a consistent and logical way. But we have seen the difficulties which societies with a written tradition come up against.

Lewis Carroll's game of 'Doublets', when played orally, turns out to be very good practice for working out the distinctive value of phonemes. For example:

Go from *black* to *bright* in the fewest possible steps, changing only one sound (not letter) each time:

>   black /blæk/
>   slack /slæk/
>   slick /slɪk/
>   slit /slɪt/
>   slight /slaɪt/
>   blight /blaɪt/
>   bright /braɪt/
> Go from *flat* to *slim*:
>   flat /flæt/
>   float /fləut/
>   gloat /gləut/
>   glut /glʌt/
>   slut /slʌt/ or glum /glʌm/
>   slit /slɪt/ or slum /slʌm/
>   slim /slɪm/ slim /slɪm/

Spoonerisms are not always the product of a slip of the tongue. Schoolchildren make deliberate use of them in 'what's the difference?' riddles such as:

Q: What's the difference between a lion with a toothache and a rainstorm?
A: Answer: one *roars* with *pain*, the other *pours* with *rain*.
Q: What's the difference between a lazy schoolboy and a fisherman?
A: One *hates* his *books* and the other *baits* his *hooks*.

Each pair of terms in these riddles—*roars/pours*; *rain/pain*; *hates/baits*; *hooks/books*—constitutes what linguists call a *minimal pair*. The process involved in creating the riddles is the same as that already described above in Chapter 4. Selecting sounds two at a time from the list of possible sounds occurring in the same context is the very process which enables us to draw up an inventory of the phonemes of a language, in other words the *distinctive* sounds. The part of linguistics which deals with phonemes is called phonemics (or phonology). Phonetics, on the other hand, deals with actual pronunciation and with *phonetic* (i.e. non-distinctive) variation—whether individual, regional, social, or contextual. This is an important, if difficult, distinction. Professor Higgins is definitely more of a phonetician than of a phonologist.

To use an analogy here, one could say that in the same way the musical code selects sounds which it deems to be 'notes' and organizes them into scales—and we know that these scales are not universal, but specific to a given culture—so each language sorts through all the sounds it is physically possible to produce with the speech organs and then assigns a number of them a place in the phonological system specific to that language.

A Flea and a Fly in a Flue: Identifying Phonemes

Every human being is born with the same sound-producing (articulatory) ability. Everyone can utter a very wide range of sounds, as is clearly shown by the 'babbling' of very young children. A baby can produce sounds which seem incredibly strange and outlandish to the people around it. Jakobson (1941) writes:

In its babble, a child can articulate an overall number of sounds which never come together in a single language, not even in a whole family of languages: consonants with vastly different points of articulation, palatal and rounded, sibilant and fricative; then there are clicks, complex vowels, diphthongs, etc.

For the child, these sounds are above all expressive, playful. Plunged into a world of meaningless sound, the child plays with its voice as though the latter were a toy or a musical instrument. The sounds are also phatic—the babble informs the child, as it were, of its own presence. At this stage, the sounds do not have communicative value: the child cannot yet organize them into messages. But then, as it learns its mother tongue—as it listens to the people around it—the baby gradually identifies some order within this sonic chaos, a system which effectively privileges certain sounds: the distinctive sounds (which *convey* but do not *contain* meaning) of the language: a language which the child, as yet, does not even realize it is learning.

Strangely enough, the child will progressively lose the ability to articulate the sounds which do not belong in this system, losing a natural ability in favour of a cultural one. What is more surprising still is that the child, in the early stage of language acquisition, loses not only those sounds which are foreign to the language it is acquiring, but also a good number of those which do belong to the system. The child recognizes them, but has to re-learn how to articulate them. Learning the distinctive value of the phonemes thus entails a temporary regression. Accordingly, from age 2 to 4, there is a gap between the child's passive competence (its ability to recognize the distinctive sounds of its language) and its active competence (its ability to reproduce them). If your child, for example, calls a sheep a 'seep', it does not mean that the child cannot hear the difference and the worst thing one can do is to start imitating the child and indulging in 'baby talk'. When the world of sound switches from being *phonetic* to being *phonological*, the child has to learn how to identify the often subtle boundaries between sounds *inasmuch* as they generate differences in meaning. The more two phonemes resemble each other, the more the child will find it difficult to keep them apart; to distinguish, for example, between *truck* and *chuck*, or *sing* and *thing*: a fact which explains why we resort, partly in a spirit of play, partly for pedagogic purposes, to the classic childrens' tongue-twisters:

She was a thistle sifter and sifted thistles through a thistle sieve

The sixth sheikh's sixth sheep's sick

I can think of six thin things and of six thick things too

Peter Piper picked a peck of pickled peppers

Around the rugged rocks the ragged rascal ran

or the following ditty:

She sells sea-shells on the sea-shore.
The shells she sells are sea-shells I am sure,
For if she sells sea-shells on the sea-shore
Then I am sure she sells sea-shore shells.

These examples bear out the fact that the opposition between neighbouring phonemes /ʃ/ as in *shell* and /s/ as in *sell* or /θ/ as in *thin* and /s/ as in *sin*, is acquired with difficulty and remains fragile. The English phoneme /r/ is also particularly difficult for young children to articulate (they usually pronounce *tchuck* or *twuck* for *truck*) and also for foreigners whose language contains a different kind of /r/ (the French) or no /r/ at all.

Tongue-twisters are found in all languages: proof that everywhere children come up against the same learning difficulties. Thus, in France, we find:

Les chaussettes de l'archiduchesse sont-elles sèches, archisèches?

or:

Un chasseur sachant chasser doit savoir chasser sans son chien.

which concerns /ʃ/ and /s/ again.

In German:

der Mondschein scheint schon schön

In Spanish:

Tres tristes tigres tragaron trigo en un trigal

In Russian:

Mishi b'egayout po krisham

etc.

The young child is extremely sensitive to minimal pairs and loves playing with paronymic sequences which bring together and juxtapose a group of very similar words. This accounts for the success, at nursery shool, of ditties such as:

A flea and a fly in a flue
Were imprisoned, so what could they do?
Said the flea, 'let us fly'
Said the fly, 'let us flee',
So, they flew through a flaw in the flue.

or:

Did you eever iver ever in your leaf life loaf
See the deevil divil devil kiss his weef wife woaf ?
No, I neever niver never in my leaf life loaf
Saw the deevil divil devil kiss his weef wife woaf.

While still young a child can acquire several foreign languages, in addition to its mother tongue, and is able to operate several different, co-existing phonological systems. As time passes, however, the child finds it increasingly difficult to hear and therefore to articulate the sounds which do not have a distinctive value in its own language.

The Phonemes of English

It is now time to look in a bit more detail at the phonemes of a particular language, English, in order to introduce some terms and concepts that will be needed for later discussion and to explain some of the less familiar symbols that are found throughout the book. The symbols come from the IPA (International Phonetic Alphabet), an alphabet which has a unique symbol for every major sound that can occur in the languages of the world. Figure

6.1 shows one possible analysis of the vowel phonemes of British Standard English (also known as 'Received Pronunciation' or 'RP'), and of 'General American' (GA) English.[6] I discuss the differences between these two later in this chapter, in the section on 'Accents of English'.

Fig. 6.1. The vowel phonemes of British (RP) and American (GA) English

	RP only	both	GA only
(a) short vowels			
ɪ		kit, bid	
ɛ		dress, bed	
æ		trap, bad	
ɒ	lot, odd		
ʌ		bud, love	
ʊ		foot, good	
(b) long vowels*			
iː		fleece, sea	
uː		goose, two	
ɑː		start, father	lot, odd
ɒː			thought, law
ɔː	thought, law	north, war	
ɜː	nurse, stir		
ɜʵː			nurse stir
(c) diphthongs**			
eɪ		face, day	
aɪ		price, high	
ɔɪ		choice, boy	
əʊ	goat, show		
oʊ			goat, show
aʊ		mouth, now	
ɪə	near, here		
ɛə	square, fair		
ʊa	poor		
(d) the 'weak' vowel (schwa)*			
ə		*a*bout, comm*a*	

 * The colon (ː) symbolizes length

 ** In contrast to the 'pure' vowels which maintain the same sound quality throughout, a diphthong starts as one vowel sound and finishes as another.

 *** /ə/ is a weak vowel variant that occurs pervasively in unstressed syllables in English. Because its occurrence is predictable from word stress it is not considered as a phoneme in its own right.

 [6] The phonology of the English vowel system is complex, and a number of alternative analyses are possible. The one presented here is somewhat simplified, but sufficient for our purposes.

The quality of a vowel, whether it is 'back' or 'high' (or 'front' or 'low') is determined by the position of the tongue relative to the roof of the mouth. The IPA system uses as a reference point a set of 'Cardinal Vowels', in which the space inside the mouth is represented diagrammatically as in Figure 6.2. The front high vowel /i/ is formed when the highest point of the tongue is near the front of the roof of the mouth while the low back vowel /ɑ/ is produced with the tongue as low and back as possible. Other vowels are articulated in intermediary positions between these two extremes. Vowels may also be either 'rounded' or 'unrounded', depending on the shape taken by the lips during their production. Thus /i/ is an unrounded vowel, whereas /u/ is a rounded vowel.

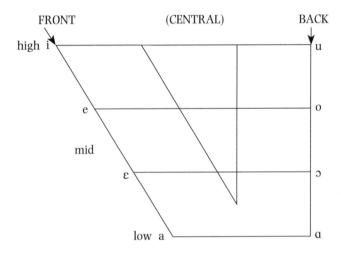

FIG. 6.2. The IPA Cardinal Vowels

Figure 6.3 shows the vowel chart for the RP English long, short, and weak vowels.

To describe systematically the way in which speech sounds are made, it is necessary to think of the mouth as a zone with two types of articulators: the upper articulators consisting of the upper lip and teeth and the roof of the mouth; and the lower articulators being the lower lip and teeth, and most importantly the tongue. Vowels differ from other speech sounds in that the upper and lower articulators are positioned far enough away from each other to allow the unrestricted passage of air between them. Consonants, on the other hand, are characterized by various degrees of stricture, from near-closure which causes turbulence (as in the fricative sounds such as /s/ and

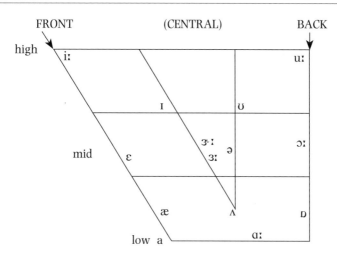

Fɪɢ. 6.3. An IPA chart of some of the vowel phonemes of English

/z/), to complete closure (as in the stops /p/ and /t/). Consonants are distinguished from one another on the basis of three major criteria:

(1) place of articulation (where the upper and lower articulators meet);
(2) manner of articulation (the degree and nature of the stricture);
(3) voice (voiceless consonants are produced with no vibration of the vocal cords, while voiced consonants are accompanied by vibration of the vocal cords during all or part of their articulation).

Figure 6.4 is a diagrammatic representation of the upper and lower articulators, showing the major areas into which they are divided, and the position of the vocal cords in relation to them. Note that the points of articulation are given their Latin rather than their English names: convention dictates that sounds are described using these terms rather than their English equivalents (when they exist), in the order 'lower articulator-upper articulator'. Thus we have terms such as 'labio-dental' (the stricture is between the lower lip and the upper teeth, as in /f/), and 'apico-alveolar' (the stricture is between the tip of the tongue and the alveolar ridge at the front of the hard palate, behind the top teeth).

Armed with the terminology, we are now in a position to look at the consonant phonemes of English, as set out in Figure 6.5. The classification is based on the articulatory scheme outlined above, and on a set of terms for different manners of articulation. The places of articulation for English consonant phonemes are:

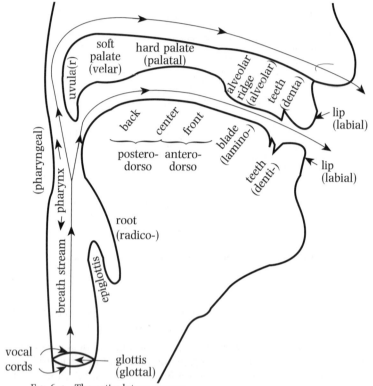

FIG. 6.4. The articulatory organs

TEACHER. To sum up, then: it takes years and years to learn how to speak properly. But thanks to science, we can do it in just a few minutes. In order to produce words, sounds and all the rest of it, you must show no mercy and drive all the air out of your lungs and then make it brush gently past your vocal chords which, harp-like, or like leaves in the breeze, start to tremble, to shake, to vibrate, to vibrate, vibrate or grate, hiss and crumple, whistle, whistle and everything starts to move: uvulum, tongue, palate, teeth . . .

PUPIL. My teeth hurt.

TEACHER. . . . lips . . . Then, at last, words start coming out of your nose, mouth, ears, pores, uprooting and hauling out along with them all the organs we were talking about, in a powerful, majestic ascent we—wrongly—call a voice. Then it becomes song, or changes into a terrible, symphonic storm, an endless stream . . . bouquets of variegated blooms, of beguiling sound: labials, dentals, stops, palatals and more, now caressing, now bitter, violent.

(Eugene Ionesco, *The Lesson*)

- bilabial: the lips come together;
- labio-dental: the lower lip touches the front teeth;
- dental: the tip of the tongue touches the upper front teeth;
- alveolar: the tip or blade of the tongue touches the alveolar ridge;
- palato-alveolar: the tip or blade of the tongue touches the alveolar ridge and the hard palate;
- palatal: the front of the tongue approaches or touches the hard palate;
- velar: the back of the tongue touches the soft palate;
- glottal: the vocal cords come together either completely as for glottal stop of partially as for /h/.

The manners of articulation are indicated in Figure 6.5 by the terms arranged vertically on the left-hand side. Where there is a contrast between a voiced and a voiceless phoneme the voiceless one comes first. The terms that we need for a description and classification of English consonant phonemes are:

- stop (or plosive): total closure, during which air pressure builds up behind the closure, followed by a sudden release;
- fricative: partial closure which forces the air through a narrow passage, creating turbulence and producing a sound of friction;
- affricate: a complex sound consisting of a stop (total closure) followed by a slow release that produces friction;
- nasal: total closure in the mouth, but the soft palate (velum) is lowered so that air escapes through the nose;
- approximants (liquids and semivowels): the articulators come close together (closer than for vowels), but not to the extent that audible friction is produced. /l/ is one of the 'lateral' sounds produced by allowing air to escape around the sides of the tongue.

Each consonant is differentiated uniquely from all others on the basis of at least one of its articulatory or voicing features. The total set of features needed to differentiate all the phonemes of English from one another are the set of *distinctive features* of the phonemic system of English. These features are based on articulatory facts but should be seen as an abstraction from them: they are terms in an abstract system of phonemic representation. Note that in the discussion above and in Figure 6.5 the term for the lower articulator is not always specified. This is because the information provided by the upper articulator and the manner of articulation is enough to distinguish the consonants from one another: the information about the lower articulator is redundant, and therefore not part of the system of distinctive features. Similarly, although /l/ is a lateral there is no need to mention this in its set of distinctive features because it is differentiated from the other liquid sound /r/ by its place of articulation.

In sharp contrast to the vowel system, which is very variable across

Fig. 6.5. The consonants of English

		bilabial	labio-dental	dental	alveolar	palato-alveolar or post-alveolar	palatal	velar	glottal
stop	voiceless	p			t			k	
	voiced	b			d			g	
fricative	voiceless		f	θ	s	ʃ			h
	voiced		v	ð	z	ʒ			
affricative	voiceless					tʃ			
	voiced					dʒ			
nasal	voiced	m			n			ŋ	
liquid	voiced				l	r			
semi-vowel	voiced	w					j		

The sounds of the consonants are exemplified below:

Stops

  p *p*an   t *t*ill   k *k*ilt
  b *b*an   d *d*ill   g *g*ilt

Fricatives

  f *f*at   θ *th*in   s *s*eal   ʃ *fa*sh*ion*   h *h*at
  v *v*at   ð *th*is   z *z*eal   ʒ *revi*si*on*

Affricates

  tʃ *ch*in
  dʒ *g*in

Nasals

  m *m*ail   n *n*ail   ŋ *si*ng

Liquids

  l *l*ap   r *r*ap

Semi-vowels

  w *w*et   j *y*et

dialects, the consonant system in English has been relatively stable. There is little significant variation, for instance, between RP and GA.

How Phonemes Vary

We have seen that the inventory of the phonemes of a language is established on the basis of their distinctive values and that linguists use so-called minimal pairs to test this.

Just as a piece of music is played differently by different musicians, so the sounds of a language can vary from one speaker to another and from one utterance to the next. But these individual variations are perceived as the 'same' sounds, as long as they retain the same distinctive value. This 'free variation' will be discussed in detail in the next section. For the time being, suffice it to say that phonemes give us a certain amount of leeway. No matter how you pronounce your r's, with an English, Scottish, or foreign accent, you will not alter the distinctive value of /r/, as long as it remains distinct from other phonemes: /l/, for example. This may be easier said than done for some foreign speakers. A Japanese speaker has great difficulty in keeping these two sounds distinct: hence the caricature 'I am velly, velly preased to meet you'.

Phonemes, however, do not vary only in isolation, but also in context. In English, /l/ is pronounced 'clear' before a vowel, and 'dark' at the end of a word: compare, for example, the two different sounds in *little*. Yet these are only variants, not different phonemes, because they are never found in the same contexts. That is, their occurrence is completely predictable and they never serve to establish a minimal pair, i.e. to distinguish between words. In Russian, however, clear /l/ and dark /ł/ do constitute distinct phonemes: they can occur in the same context in distinct words. Another example of predictable variation is found with /p/ in English, which is usually accompanied by a small puff of air (aspiration). Yet this aspiration does not occur after /s/. Speakers are not aware of pronouncing the /p/ sound of *pit* and *spit* differently as the variants are produced automatically in the appropriate context. By contrast, in Bengali, Chinese, and Swahili, aspirated /pʰ/ and unaspirated /p/ *are* opposed: they serve to differentiate words and are thus different phonemes.

Contextual and individual variation is *phonetic*, not *phonological*. Consequently, a phoneme can be defined as *a group of sounds around a nucleus possessing the same distinctive value in a given language*. Borrowing a concept from modern mathematics, we might say that a phoneme is a 'fuzzy set'. Just as a morpheme has allomorphs, so a phoneme has *allophones*. What matters is not so much the physical quality of the sound produced, as the distance separating phonemes from each other within the phonological system. Phonetics is the science of the actual, concrete sounds of language. The phonetic alphabet tends to represent not only phonemes but also their major allophones, such as 'dark' and 'clear' l. This is sometimes called a 'narrow' transcription. By convention a phonetic transcription uses square brackets: thus dark l [ł] is opposed to clear l [l]. A phonemic or 'broad' transcription, on the other hand, will disregard allophonic variation and will therefore use fewer symbols. The phoneme symbols are enclosed between slanting lines or virgules: /l/. It is important to realize that the phoneme is an abstract construct: /l/ is an abstraction over the phonetic 'reality' of [l] versus [ł].

A simile can be drawn with the musical scale. Variations also occur, the notion of 'in tune' being a relative one: a traditionally tuned harpsichord, for example, has a slightly different range from the contemporary scale. Indeed, in the past, the musical scale varied from one instrument to another, from one country to another. But the *intervals* between notes remained the same: as, therefore, did their individual distinctive values.

Foreign Accents and Distinctive Features

Having an 'accent' in a foreign language stems, precisely, from attempting to replace a phoneme of the foreign language with the phoneme in one's native language which is closest to it. In English, the phoneme /t/, for example, is distinguished from /d/ by one feature only, which is that of *voicing*: /d/ is pronounced with vibration of the vocal chords, /t/ is not and is called 'voiceless'. Now, in German, /d/ is de-voiced in certain positions and is therefore not distinguished from /t/. In these circumstances, the opposition is said to be 'neutralized'. Thus, *Rad* ('bike') and *Rat* ('council') have exactly the same pronunciation, with a voiceless consonant, whereas English opposes *ride* and *rite*. Hence the caricature of a German accent—in all the films portraying Nazis, for example—where all the /d/ sounds are replaced by /t/, and conversely. The opposite phenomenon arises in English when /t/ becomes voiced between vowels, as in the American pronunciation of *city* [sidi], or *latter*, which then becomes identical to *ladder*.

The French are notorious for their inability to pronounce the English TH, whether voiced /ð/ as in *this* or voiceless /θ/ as in *thin*. These two TH sounds are pronounced with ze tip of ze tongue, or rather, with the tip of the tongue between the teeth and thus resemble, on the one hand, /s/ and /z/ (pronounced with the tongue pressed against the alveolar ridge—see Figures 6.3 and 6.4), and, on the other hand, /f/ and /v/ (which are pronounced with the lips and the teeth). All three pairs of consonants are fricatives: that is, they share the same mode of articulation—partially blocking the stream of air, thus causing friction. A French accent consists, therefore, of pronouncing *this* as [zis] or [vis], that is keeping the same *mode* of articulation, but shifting the *place* of articulation. Speakers of Germanic languages often replace the same TH, voiced or voiceless, with /t/ or /d/, which have the same *place* of articulation, but a different *mode* of articulation: they are stops, which means that when they are pronounced, the stream of air is blocked and then suddenly released (see Figures 6.3 and 6.4). The same phenomenon is observed in English-based pidgins and creoles as well as in Cockney and in Black English vernaculars. It is reminiscent of some of the sound changes that happened in the early Germanic languages. We find a systematic correspondence between the stops of German and Dutch and the fricatives of English. Thus, *the mother* is *die Mutter* and *De moeder* in German and in Dutch, respectively; *the father* becomes *der Vatter* and *de vaeder*.[7]

---

[7] The 19th-cent. reconstitution of the links between the Indo-European languages was based on facts of this kind.

In the same vein, the caricature of a Spanish accent consists of inverting *b* and *v*, since the opposition between /b/ and /v/ is not relevant in Spanish, whereas it is in French, a related language, and—obviously—in English. In Latin, the fricative /v/ did not exist. It developed later from /b/, the stop which uses the same point of articulation. The French word for 'book'— *livre*—comes from Latin *liber*.

As far as English speakers are concerned, they often find it very difficult to pronounce the rounded vowels of French and to distinguish between *sûr* and *sourd*, since the vowels /y/ and /u/ have the same phonetic characteristics, except for rounding—a feature English lost during the *Great Vowel Shift* in the fifteenth century (the IPA system uses /y/ for a close, front, rounded vowel).

The nasal vowels, of French or Portuguese, say, can also cause problems, since many languages simply do not have them. They are only distinguished from the corresponding oral vowels by the fact that air passes through the nose, whereas, for oral vowels, air is prevented from going through the nose by the raising of the soft palate or velum.

When the nasal cavity is blocked—when we are suffering from a cold, for example—the nasal *consonants* in words like *mummy* or *not*, cannot be correctly pronounced: instead we end up saying *bubby* and *dot*, that is we produce the nearest oral consonant. The anonymous author of the followigg poeb certadly debobstrates these sybtobs:

> Chilly Dovebber with his boadigg blast
> Dow cubs add strips the bedow add the lawd
> Eved October's suddy days are past
> Add Subber's gawd![8]

When moving from one language to another, the absence of the same *phonological* contrasts causes us to substitute the nearest *phonetic* realizations from our own language, playing on one or the other of the two types of variation: *manner of articulation* (stop, fricative, affricate), or *place of articulation* (from the lips to the velum: see Figure 6.4), as well as exploiting the binary opposition between voiced and voiceless consonants.

It seems to be the case that children throughout the world, when acquiring their phonological system, first learn the vowels and consonants which are common to all languages of the world, acquiring last of all the phonemes which are the most peculiar to their own language. The first vowel acquired is an open vowel /a/, followed by a close, front vowel /i/, then a close, back vowel /u/ (see Figure 6.6). These three form the minimal system in most if not all languages, the other vowels taking up their positions in relation to these, in virtually infinite variety from language to language.

---

[8] From J. M. Cohen (ed.), *Belagcholly Days: A Choice of Comic and Curious Verse* (London: Penguin, 1975), 237.

I   u

a

FIG. 6.6. Minimal vocalic system

In a process parallel to the one just described, the first consonants acquired are stops and labials—pronounced using the lips (perhaps connected to a baby's natural sucking movement?)—and the first meaningful distinction acquired is generally that between nasal consonants (/m/) and oral consonants (/p/, /b/); the second is the one which separates labials (/p/, /b/, /m/) from dentals (/t/, /d/, /n/). We recognize straightaway the initial consonants of the first words produced by children all over the world: *mummy, daddy*; maman, papa (French); *matuska, bat'uska* (Russian); *mama, tata* (Serbo-Croat), etc.[9]

This order of acquisition is exactly reversed in the gradual loss of language which affects aphasics. The sounds which had been acquired first resist the illness longest.[10]

Sound Change and its Consequences:

The status of a phoneme is not established once and for all. Languages are constantly evolving and the system constantly undergoes redefinition.

There are two kinds of change which can take place: *chain shifts*, on the one hand, and *splits* and *mergers*, on the other.

Chain shifts work rather like musical chairs or the guests moving around the table at the Mad Hatter's tea-party. The best known example of this is the *Great Vowel Shift* which affected the English vowel system around the end of the fifteenth century—broadly speaking between the ages of Chaucer and Shakespeare. All long vowels became significantly more closed, which had the effect of driving out the two most closed vowels of the original system /i:/ (front) and /u:/ (back): this in turn caused two dipthongs to appear, /ai/ and /aʊ/, which produced changes in pronunciation of the following kind:

Middle English /staːn/ ⟩ Modern English /stəun/ *stone*
Middle English /goːs/ ⟩ Modern English /guːs/ *goose*
Middle English /huːs/ ⟩ Modern English /haʊs/ *house*
Middle English /geːs/ ⟩ Modern English /giːs/ *geese*
Middle English /miːn/ ⟩ Modern English /maɪn/ *mine*

In this revised model, the same phonemic distinctions are maintained in a different form and the whole system is redefined with no loss of communicative potential.

[9] Cf. Jakobson (1960*b*).   [10] Cf. Jakobson (1941).

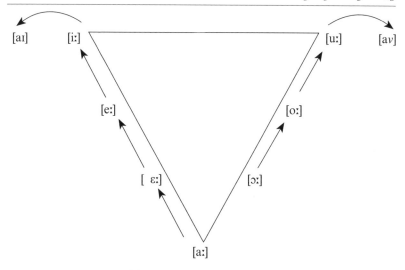

Fig. 6.7. Diagram of the Great Vowel Shift

In the case of splits or mergers, the system is only partially affected.

Splits end up creating new oppositions: former allophones become distinct phonemes. They allow the suppression of homophones by changing them into minimal pairs. One such split affected the short /u/ of English in the seventeenth century, resulting in such pairs as *look/luck, could/cud*, which were previously homophones (and still are in many northern dialects of modern English). Another example is that of fricative consonants. In Old English voiced and unvoiced fricatives [v, f], [ð, θ], and [z, s] were allophones of *three* phonemes, with the voiced variants appearing between vowels. In Modern English we find *six* phonemes, allowing us to distinguish such minimal pairs as *relieve/relief, wreathe/wreath*, or *devise/device*.

In *mergers*, on the contrary, new homophones result from the fusion of minimal pairs. Certain *lexical sets* which used to be distinct, no longer are. This is what happened between the fifteenth and seventeenth centuries when Middle English /i/, /ə/, and /u/ were all merged before /r/, which produced such homophonic pairs as *berth/birth, earn/urn, purl/pearl, surf/serf*. Hence the possibility of the excruciating: 'What's a Greek urn?' 'Oh, about a hundred quid a week.'

Mergers, therefore, obviously risk creating ambiguity, in which language is already saturated. But, as we saw earlier, ambiguity is limited, fortunately, by the distribution of homophones between different syntactic classes.

Accents of English

Different dialects of English have different histories of splits, mergers and shifts in their systems. The result is what we call 'accent'.

From a purely *descriptive* point of view, accents vary in three different ways. First, there are *phonemic* differences when one dialect has two phonemes where another has only one. For instance in Scottish English *pool* and *pull* or *fool* and *full* are homophones, whereas they are minimal pairs in most other accents. Some American speakers use the same vowel in *cot* and *caught*. Second, there are *phonetic* differences between dialects that maintain the same distinctions between phonemes but pronounce them differently. Speakers of Scottish English use a 'flap' [ɾ] for their /r/ phoneme that is very strikingly different from British or American English but it definitely serves the same function in the system (i.e. it occurs in the same words). Or again the British diphthong /əʊ/, as in *home*, becomes /oʊ/ or /o/ in American.

Lastly, the distribution of phonemes in the lexicon may vary: Americans pronounce *ask* or *dance* (but not *father* or *palm*) with the vowel of *cat*. North of England speakers who distinguish *pull* and *pool* may have a long vowel in *cook* where RP has a short one. There is also a certain amount of free variation.

You say /təmeɪtəʊ / and I say /təmaːtəʊ/   (tomato)
You say /iːθər/ and I say /aɪθər/   (either)

Here are some more examples of accent variation:

Merry Mary, will you marry me?

Across the different dialects of English, we meet all possible combinations of the pronunciation of the three words *merry*, *Mary*, *marry*: all three rhyme, two of them rhyme, or none at all (see Figure 6.8[11] below for examples).

Standard British RP	[mɛri] ≠ [mɛ əri] ≠ [mæri]
Scottish	[mɛ ri] ≠ [mɛri] ≠ [mari]
General American	[mɛ ri] = [mɛ ri] = [mɛ ri] *or* ≠ [mæri]
Southern US	[mɛ ri] ≠ [meiri] ≠ [mæri]
Philadelphia	[mʌri] ≠ [mɛ ri] = [mɛ ri]

The three types of variation occur here. British RP has an extra phoneme in Mary. The other differences are either phonetic or distributional.

Fɪɢ. 6.8. Merry, Mary, marry

[11] Based on Wells (1982).

It sounds like a horse, Alice thought to herself. And an extremely small voice, close to her ear, said 'you might make a joke on that—something about "horse" and "hoarse", you know'. (131)

This pun from *Through the Looking Glass*, playing on the fact that *horse* and *hoarse* are identical in Standard British English, is lost on Scots, who make a distinction between the two words.

Q: Why is a chef like a journalist?
A: Because both refuse to reveal their [sɔ:siz] (sources = sauces).

The homophony exploited by this little riddle is not valid for all speakers of English. It will only work for those who do not pronounce /r/ after a vowel, as has been the case in Standard British English since the eighteenth century. But for most Americans *sauce* and *source* constitute a minimal pair. The Mock Turtle makes a similar pun when he says to Alice, 'We called him Tortoise because he taught us' (75).

For the same reason, the poem by Edgar Allan Poe, *The Raven*, whose refrain is *nevermore*, will not have the same effect on a Briton as on an American. Indeed, Poe himself underlined how much the final *r*—'the most producible consonant'—contributed to the resonance and evocative force of the word.

In fact, the presence or absence of a post-vocalic /r/ divides English dialects very clearly into two groups, a division which is linked not to geography, but to the way the English language spread throughout history. The division is between what are called *rhotic* (General American, Scottish, Irish, etc.) and *non-rhotic* (British RP, also called 'BBC English' or 'Oxford English', Australian, Black English Vernacular, New York, Boston, etc.) dialects. The loss of post-vocalic /r/ has the effect of increasing the number of vocalic phonemes in non-rhotic dialects (see Figures 6.2 and 6.3 for a comparison of standard British and American systems).

Accents and Prejudice

Within the English-speaking community, accent is a powerful discriminator of ethnic, geographical, and social origin. It should not be confused with dialect, which is defined in terms of grammar and lexicon. Standard English is spoken with all kinds of regional or social accents. Regional dialects, however, are most commonly associated with a specific accent. Although it is theoretically possible to speak any dialect with any accent, the Received Pronunciation of English (RP) is only used by speakers of standard English. Hence the comic effect produced when Eliza, in *Pygmalion*, mimics impeccable RP while still using Cockney grammar.[12]

---

[12] *Pygmalion*, Act III.

Accent variation, indeed, gives rise to all sorts of prejudice. Some favourable, some unfavourable. Curiously, speaking with a post-vocalic /r/, the norm in General American (spoken throughout the USA except the East Coast and the South), is considered prestigious in New York, where it marks the speech of the upper classes: but RP, the most prestigious British accent, does not have a post-vocalic /r/.

" Please, Ma'am, you've dropped something."

Dropping 'aitches', a much stigmatized habit, is one of the most prominent characteristics of Cockney English and is found, in fact, in most working class accents of Britain. It makes possible such puns as:

'What are [boots and shoes] made of?' Alice asked in a tone of great curiosity.
'Soles and eels, of course,' the Gryphon replied. (81)

As a linguistic feature, this was often put down to laziness in articulation, something which J. C. Wells—the best known specialist of English dialects—contests:

The fact that Northumbrians, Scots, Irish, Americans and Barbadians do not incline to H dropping is sufficient proof, if proof were needed, that there is no truth in the popular English view that H dropping is a product of laziness and original sin. Or are there no lazy Americans?[13]

Anything is possible in this area, but everything is relative.

Some languages, e.g. Serbo-Croatian, use very few vowels in their spelling system because they do not transcribe 'neutral' vowels. This gives the (wrong) impression of a vowel-less language. Others, on the contrary, seem to have an overabundant supply of vowels. The piece of satire in the box was posted by Mark R. Gover on the *Language Use list* shortly after the end of the war in Bosnia.

CLINTON DEPLOYS VOWELS TO BOSNIA

Cities of Sjlbvdnzv, Grzny to Be First Recipients

Before an emergency joint session of Congress yesterday, President Clinton announced US plans to deploy over 75,000 vowels to the war-torn region of Bosnia. The deployment, the largest of its kind in American history, will provide the region with the critically needed letters A, E, I, O and U, in the hope of rendering countless Bosnian names more pronounceable.

'For six years, we have stood by while names like Ygrjvslhv and Tzlynhr and Glrm have been horribly butchered by millions around the world,' Clinton said. 'Today, the United States must finally stand up and say, "Enough." It is time the people of Bosnia finally had some vowels in their words. The US is proud to lead the crusade in this noble endeavour.'

The deployment, dubbed 'Operation Vowel Storm' by the State Department, is set for early next week, with the Adriatic port cities of Sjlbvdnzv and Grzny slated to be the first recipients. Two C-130 transport planes, each carrying over 500 24-count boxes of 'E's,' will fly from Andrews Air Force Base across the Atlantic and airdrop the letters over the cities.

Citizens of Grzny and Sjlbvdnzv eagerly await the arrival of the vowels. 'I do not think we can last another day,' Trszg Grzdnjkln, 44, said. 'I have six children and none of them has a name that is understandable to me or to anyone else. Mr. Clinton, please send my poor, wretched family just one "E." Please.'

Said Sjlbvdnzv resident Grg Hmphrs, 67: 'With just a few key letters, I could be George Humphries. This is my dream.'

The airdrop represents the largest deployment of any letter to a foreign country since 1984. During the summer of that year, the US shipped 92,000 consonants to Ethiopia, providing cities like Ouaouoaua, Eaoiiuae, and Aao with vital, life-giving supplies of L's, S's and T's.

(Mark R. Gover in a post to the *Language use* mailing list)

---

[13] Wells (1982): i. 256.

7   Words as Signs

> Having discovered the world through language, for a long time I mistook language for the world
>
> (Jean-Paul Sartre, *Words*)

Balnibarbi : Words and Things

In his book *The Order of Things* the French philosopher Michel Foucault argues that reality only exists insofar as it is *named*. Indeed, we are all accustomed to thinking that things have a name: we use expressions like, 'call things by their name', 'call a spade, a spade'. While walking through the wood where things have no name, Alice finds herself to be suffering from amnesia and is consequently no longer able to understand the reality around her, or to indulge in abstract thought. In another episode, when the gnat asks her if insects answer to their names, she replies, 'I never knew them do it.' 'What's the use of their having names,' the gnat says, 'if they won't answer to them?' Alice continues, 'No use to *them* . . . but it's useful to the people that name them, I suppose. If not why do they have names at all?' (132).

But giving something a name is not the same as putting labels on objects, as the Academicians of Balnibarbi seem to think in Swift's *Gulliver's Travels*. They suggest replacing words—which have the disadvantage of differing from one language to another—by objects which one could carry around on one's back and use for communication. Apart from the obvious practical disadvantage of such a system, an object would be quite unable to indicate—simply by virtue of its physical reality—the properties it possesses, or its membership of a class of objects, or whether it was countable or uncountable, present in, or absent from the context of communication: language, indeed, does not require objects to be present in order to refer to them, nor even that the objects exist. For, linguistic activity is *symbolic* activity. Language serves as a vehicle for thought, which links concepts: it does not consist of labels which have simply been stuck on things. To name, in other words, is at the same time to *categorize*, to organize the world. Words have the power to form concepts: the word actually creates the concept just as much as the concept necessitates the word. Any new activity, new idea, or new reality requires to be named, but it is this very naming process which gives it an existence in the conceptual world of speakers.

If one ignores its expression in words, our thought is no more than an indistinct, amorphous mass. Philosophers and linguists have always agreed that, without the help of signs, we would be unable to keep different ideas apart in a clear and consistent way. . . . There are no pre-established ideas and there are no distinctions prior to the appearance of language.[1]

The words of a language constitute an autonomous system, quite independent from the things they name. I return to a detailed discussion of this important point in the next chapter.

Signs—since that is what words are—are defined *in relation to each other*. One sign can always be restated using other signs, either within the same code (through synonymy, paraphrase, or dictionary definition), or by transposing it into a different code, as in the case of translation: but the very difficulty of the latter demonstrates that there is no simple, self-evident, one-to-one relationship between words and things.

One famous OULIPO[2] exercise illustrates the relationship between the words in a language. The exercise consists of taking a sentence and replacing each of its words with its dictionary definition or paraphrase. The operation is recursive—that is, it can be repeated as many times as one wishes. Here is an example of what can be produced.

Cleopatra's nose: had it been shorter, the whole face of the Earth would have changed.

First stage:

The pointed part of the face of an Egyptian queen famous for her beauty: had it been less long, the whole face of the planet inhabited by man would have moved from one state to another.

Second stage:

The portion which sticks out, of the face of the wife of the king of a northeast African republic, famous for her physical, moral, or artistic harmony: had it been less extended from one end to the other, the whole face of the non-luminous heavenly body on which the human race makes its home would have gone from one manner of being to another.

---

[1] Saussure ([1915] 1959).

[2] OULIPO—an acronym for *Ouvroir de littérature potentielle* ('Workshop of Potential Literature')- is a literary group, established among others by Raymond Queneau, Italo Calvino, George Perec, and Harry Matthews, dedicated to searching for new, unexploited literary forms, and creating bizarre, unexpected, but always original and interesting modes of expression.

Third stage:

> The part which grows forwards from the face of the companion of the head of a state in which the people exercise sovereignty through delegates elected by them, a state situated between the north and the east of one of the five parts of the world, renowned for her material science of chords, concerning customs or having a connection with the arts: if it had had less size from one end to the other, the whole face of the star which gives out no light on which the genus of man forms its home would have moved from one extreme to the other.

As we define or replace each word with a synonym or a paraphrase, we stress the interdependence between the new terms and the original ones but at the same time we move further and further away from the meaning of the original message because every step introduces some form of differentiation.

The Parrot: Signifier, Signified and Referent

In his celebrated *Course in General Linguistics*, published posthumously in 1915, the Swiss linguist Ferdinand de Saussure was the first person to define the linguistic sign as a double-sided entity: on one side the *signifier*, the sound sequence which constitutes its physical reality; on the other, the *signified*, that is the idea or the concept that the signifier evokes. The signifier *dog*, for example, the sound sequence represented phonetically by [dɔg], does not evoke a particular dog with all its individual characteristics, but rather the notion of 'dog', the general, abstract idea, with a classificatory value, which takes no account of different breeds of dog, nor of their different sizes, properties, colours, and so on. The word *dog* in the English language establishes a category of 'dog-ness'.

More importantly, the signifier and the signified are the *inseparable* constituents of the sign and one must avoid the common error which consists in believing that the signifier *is* the word and the signified is the reality which it designates. It is the sign with *both* its sides which, as an element within the autonomous system of language, allows us as speakers, when we use it in a sentence, to *refer* to the extra-linguistic world, whether real or imaginary, abstract or concrete, near or distant, known or unknown. The sign, in other words, is *independent* of what it refers to, the *referent*. Indeed, outside a particular utterance, the sign has no referent, but only has a sense or value which is defined in relation to the value of the other signs in the system. Put metalinguistically, the sign is auto-referential: it refers to itself (see, in Chapter 1, 'The Word "Dog" does not Bark'). Moreover, since numerous signifieds can correspond to the same signifier, contextual meaning is always the result of the association *between the sign and the referent* within a given utterance. A sentence has, once uttered, both a meaning and a referent. The criterion of truth can only be applied to utterances and not to individual words.

Examples in school grammars point up an interesting phenomenon: meaning and reference may diverge. A well-known example from Latin grammar will illustrate the point:

hortus est Petro
garden is Peter + dative
a garden is to Peter = 'Peter has a garden'

Clearly, *hortus est Petro* refers neither to an owner called *Peter* nor to his garden, but simply to the rule for expressing possession directed at school-children.

Meaning can be deliberately divorced from reference as in these verses recited in lieu of evidence by the White Rabbit at the end of the mock-trial:

> They told me you had been to her,
> And mentioned me to him:
> She gave me a good character,
> But said I could not swim.
>
> He sent them words I had not gone
> (We know it to be true):
> If she should push the matter on,
> What would become of you?
>
> I gave her one, they gave him two,
> You gave us three or more;
> They all returned from him to you,
> Though they were mine before.
>
> . . .

Alice is quite mistaken when she exclaims: 'I don't believe there's any atom of meaning in it.' For the pronouns obviously have meaning. What they lack is reference, and this makes the verses *uninterpretable*.

The charming fable of the parrot told by Jean Paulhan in *Le Don des langues* ('The Gift of Languages'), demonstrates this triple relationship between signifier/signified/ referent. Three people are studying parrots. The first takes into account only the form of the word 'parrot', its phonetic evolution through history and notes down its cognates, synonyms, and equivalents in other languages. The second person considers only the signified, what is evoked by the word, what its semantic field is, the metaphors, symbolic or figurative uses made of it, the associations or connotations which attach to it. The third person devotes himself to the study of the object, the parrot, the different species of parrots throughout the world. None of the three ever stops to think that his vision of the problem is only partial.

Charles and Lucinda, Sharon and Darren: The Problem of Proper Names

Are proper names also signs? This is the question Lewis Carroll raises in the chapter of *Through the Looking Glass* in which Alice meets Humpty Dumpty. This is what Alice answers when he asks her to state her name and occupation:

'My *name* is Alice, but ——'
'It's a stupid name enough! . . . What does it mean?'
'*Must* a name mean something?' asked Alice doubtfully.
'Of course it must,' Humpty Dumpty said with a short laugh: 'my name means the shape I am—and a good handsome shape it is, too. With a name like yours, you might be any shape, almost.' (160)

Proper names appear to establish a direct relation between a signifier and a referent (a sound sequence and the person referred to) without going via a signified. There is no concept of 'Alice-ness' which corresponds to the signifier Alice. Proper names are not signs, or so it would seem, since signs cannot exist outside the relation signifier/signified. And yet, proper names 'include elements of gender, exoticism, regional origin, membership of a certain social class, rarity and so on'.[3]

Here, we are squarely in the domain of *connotation or associative meaning*, which makes us perceive Lucinda or Charles, say, as socially exclusive, while Sharon and Darren are seen as very much more downmarket. It is social connotations such as these which govern the choice of the names we give to children, or the judgements we form about certain family names.

Even if a proper name originally had a precise meaning (which is practically always the case, since many proper names were originally nicknames), the name, by virtue of its function, undergoes semantic 'bleaching', precisely because it is no longer required to signify. Note that some names like *Blubberguts*, or *Four-eyes*, resist bleaching much better, for example, than *Fletcher* or *Cooper*. A proper name only really becomes a sign when it becomes a common noun through the process known as metonymy, as in *balaclava, boycott, mackintosh, sandwich, wellington*, and so on. (See Chapter 12 for a more detailed discussion of metonymy.)

[3] Cf. W. Godzich (1974).

Asterix in Britain: Language and Reality

The difficulty of translating from one language into another—although the reality being talked about remains the same—results from the fact that different languages divide reality up in different ways. This fact, which highlights the autonomy of language, is rather difficult to accept since 'For the speaking subject, his/her language is totally appropriate to reality: signs map onto reality and control it, in fact they *are* reality'.[4] This is true of speakers of every language. The problem is that:

> Language is an instrument for ordering the world and society, it is applied to a world considered as 'real' and also *reflects* this 'real' world. But in this sense, each language is specific and asserts the world in its own peculiar way.[5]

At the beginning of the century, the French anthropologist Lévy-Bruhl attempted to demonstrate that the languages of so-called primitive peoples lacked abstract or generic words and that, consequently, they lent themselves only to concrete thought. The argument was based on the fact that where English or French, for example, use a single term, a given African or American language uses several—Eskimos talking of snow, Arabs of horses, or the pronouns of Amerindian or Pacific languages—whence a so-called inaptitude for generalization. But Lévy-Bruhl had quite simply forgotten carefully to analyse Indo-European languages. Had he done so he would have observed that, in many instances, the opposite holds true.

---

[4] Benveniste (1966: 52).   [5] Ibid. 82.

Let us consider a few examples. While Malagasy has several words which correspond to *we*, or to the demonstratives *this* and *that*—taking into account such things as relative distance or visibility—it only has a single word for all those dishes which can be eaten with rice, and only one word for all types of shelter, of receptacle, of house, of container, with no account taken of size or use and no distinction made between animate or inanimate, human or non-human contents. In short, there is only a single word for 'a place or object capable of containing someone or something'. This is an abstract idea which can only be rendered, in English or in French, after lengthy explanation.[6] And yet, Malagasy can also provide the means of distinguishing between *beehive, box, case, coffin, dwelling, hut, lair,* and so on, when needed. By gathering all these objects together under one common label, the language simply categorizes what they share, leaving to one side those differences which are not conceptually relevant. And it is precisely because languages differ in this way that they cannot be 'copied' from reality or, indeed, copied from one another. Hence the challenge of translation.

Many languages have classifiers for nouns. Wolof (the main language of Senegal), for instance, uses different determiners for human beings (*ki*), animals (*wi*), trees (*gi*), artefacts (*bi*), etc., thus allocating to each noun an indication of what category it belongs to. This type of conceptual labelling is not found in all languages. Indeed, even in 'classifier' languages, classification often responds to some formal constraint, in addition to the conceptual distinction. Thus in the case of the Wolof classifiers, semantic criteria intersect with formal criteria: quite often, the initial consonant of nouns is duplicated in the initial consonant of the classifier, e.g. *garab gi*, 'the tree', *guy gi*, 'the baobab', *jigeen ji*, 'the woman', *jabaar ji*, 'the wife', etc. In the same sort of way, French feels the need to label all nouns as feminine or masculine. But this classification, non-existent in many languages, has little more than a symbolic value, in French, when applied to inanimate objects.[7] Outside the sphere of human reference, gender is based on morphological rather than semantic criteria. Thus, classes within the systems of signs may be drawn in terms of formal features which have little or no connection to 'natural' distinctions in the world of referents.

Indo-European languages have only one first-person plural pronoun—*we/us*. This pronoun is not marked for gender. Nonetheless we are able to refer to relationships which, in terms of the extra-linguistic reality, are as diverse as: *me and you, me and all of you, me and you two, me and him, me and those two, me and all of them, we two and you, we two and you two, we two and all of you, we two and him, we two and them, we two and those two*. If one then adds to this list *me, a woman* and *you, a woman, me, a man* and *you, a man*,

---

[6] See Jean Paulhan, *La Mentalité primitive* (1956), 147.

[7] For examples and a discussion, see Yaguello (1978) and (1989).

me, a woman and *you, a man*, and so on, the reader will understand what I am getting at. Without being in the slightest bit aware of it, when we say *us*, this *us* can refer to an infinity of possible utterance situations. It would be extremely cumbersome and impractical to use different pronouns for each possible combination of speaker + addressee + third party (not to mention sex distinctions) even though some languages are a lot more specific in this area than English or French. Many languages have two pronouns where English only has one, pronouns which account for *some* of the differences which I have just been referring to: for example, Malagasy, Australian, Amerindian, or Philippine languages. These languages distinguish between an 'inclusive' *us*—which includes the addressee—and an 'exclusive' *us*—*ex*cluding the addressee, but *in*cluding a third party. This distinction has found its way into English-based pidgins: for example, Neo-Melanesian where we find the opposition *miyu/mipela* (⟨ *me* + *you* ≠ *me* + *my fellow*). Other languages allow for a distinction between a male and a female speaker.[8] None of this means, of course, that English speakers are incapable of *imagining* such distinctions, but simply that their language subsumes them under a common signifier, linked to a single concept: *us* = 'a group of people, of unspecified number and sex, which includes the speaker'.

Ignorance concerning the autonomous operation of language and misunderstandings about the difference between what is linguistic and what is extra-linguistic, have been used to justify racist considerations about the supposed inferiority of 'primitive' languages and peoples. Thus although the general and the particular or the abstract and the concrete—for reasons quite opaque to us—are distributed differently through languages, this cannot be the basis for value judgements about languages.[9]

The Sapir–Whorf Hypothesis

The idea that divisions within language do not correspond to divisions in reality gave rise to what is known as the Sapir–Whorf hypothesis (named after the two American linguists who developed it). In its most extreme form—now challenged by most linguists—it postulates that a speaker's view of the world is entirely determined by the structure of his/her language. This hypothesis is founded mainly on the classification of kinship terms, on the way the continuum of the colour spectrum is divided up, or on certain distinctive grammatical categories, such as tense and aspect.

[8] See R. Lakoff (1975) and Yaguello (1978).
[9] As early as 1925, Jean Paulhan in *La Mentalité primitive* denounced the illusion of superiority in Indo-European languages and cultures, which is founded on an apparent aptitude for generalization and abstraction. I have borrowed the example of Malagasy from him.

According to Whorf (1956):

the grammar of each language is not merely a reproducing instrument for voicing ideas but rather is itself the shaper of ideas, the program and guide for the individual's mental activity. . . . Formulation of ideas is not an independent process, strictly rational in the old sense, but is part of a particular grammar, and differs, from slightly to greatly, between different grammars. *We dissect nature along lines laid down by our native language.* The categories and types that we isolate from the world of phenomena we do not find there because they stare every observer in the face; on the contrary, *the world is presented in a kaleidoscopic flux of impressions which has to be organized by our minds—and this means largely by the linguistic system in our minds.* (emphasis mine)

Arguing along the same lines, Benveniste (1966) writes

It can be seen that mental categories and the rules governing thought do no more than reflect, to a very large extent, the organization and distribution of linguistic categories. . . . Varieties of philosophical and spiritual experience depend, unconsciously, on a classification imposed by language, simply because it is language and because it symbolizes. We conceive of a universe which has already been modelled by language.

Taking to its extreme the idea that language shapes thought and culture, the so-called Sapir and Whorf hypothesis posits that:

(1) speakers of languages which make certain lexical distinctions are better able to speak about the part of reality concerned, than speakers of languages which do not make these distinctions. Let us consider an example of lexical diversity which has acquired the status of a myth[10] in linguistics, that of the Eskimo words for snow. Originally it was the anthropologist Franz Boas who noted that Eskimo languages have four distinct word-roots for snow, yielding a large number of specific context-related terms, because these languages are agglutinative. The information was then highlighted by Whorf and vastly exaggerated in subsequent quotations. Such diversity is in any case neither surprising nor particularly interesting: surely, for people living in the Arctic circle, it is essential to be able to describe such a basic feature of their environment as snow with maximum accuracy. After all, English has a number of words to name different kinds of rain. A stronger claim is that lexical distinctions influence the perception of reality: for example, the perception of colours, or of kinship relations. This idea prompted to George Orwell one of the principles of Newspeak in his novel *1984*. In Newspeak, it is impossible to think of freedom or love or peace because the words do not exist. However, this relationship between lexicon and cognition can be seen as a chicken and egg situation. Indeed, one could argue that language *reflects* certain

[10] See Pullum (1991: 159–74).

cognitive categories or socio-cultural facts, as much as it sustains or imposes them. Language also changes under the pressure of social or cultural factors, and is not driven solely by an internal logic in total isolation from society.

(2) the grammatical structure of languages predisposes speakers to certain thought patterns. Thus it is suggested that English speakers are more inductive and French speakers are more deductive, since adjectives precede nouns in English, but follow them in French. The Hopi Indians allegedly have a different perception of time because their verbal system emphasizes aspect—the way in which actions are performed—to the detriment of tense. This is highly debatable. A lot of languages do without the formal category of tense. Their speakers manage perfectly well to convey time reference via aspect and adverbials. In Wolof, a language with which I am quite familiar, when speakers use the imperfective aspect with a verb denoting an action, they usually imply that it is taking place at the time of speaking, unless otherwise suggested by context.

The Sapir–Whorf hypothesis has come under attack[11] from the 'universalist' tendency, which postulates, on the contrary, that identical perceptual and cognitive operations underlie what are essentially superficial differences. But there is no denying these surface differences are to some extent the means of cultural conditioning: linguistic categories do shape the mind and the way we perceive the world via *stereotypes* and *prototypes*, and this is what can breed prejudice of every possible kind. It is also the means of feeding ideology into discourse. The struggle of the feminist movement or of various ethnic minorities against 'sexist' or 'racist' language has no other grounds. Although the strong version of the Sapir–Whorf hypothesis is no longer tenable, we must take a balanced view of the relationship between language, cognition, and the world.

---

[11] Sapir, in spite of all this controversy, will go down in history as a most respectable linguist. It is Whorf, an amateur who tended to jump to hasty (and hazy) conclusions from unverified data, whose reputation has suffered.

8 A Rose by Any Other Name
Are Signs Arbitrary or Motivated?

'*I* call it purring, not growling', said Alice. 'Call it what you like', said the cat.

(Lewis Carroll)

What's in a name? That which we call a rose by any other name would smell as sweet.

(Shakespeare, *Romeo and Juliet*)

The Arbitrary Nature of the Sign

As we have just seen, the link between sound and meaning, between signifier and signified, is a purely conventional one, because it is cultural. And yet, for the speakers of any given language, since words map onto reality, the idea that the link between the two sides of the linguistic sign is not natural and cannot be taken for granted, is rather difficult to accept. The fact is well illustrated by the following Jewish anecdote:

Daddy, says his son to the Rabbi, what we're eating, why is it called spaghetti?— Well now, son, think. Is it not white like spaghetti? Is it not long like spaghetti? Is it not soft like spaghetti? How could we not call it spaghetti?

Saussure defined the link between the signifier and the signified as *arbitrary*, or unmotivated; a link, that is, which cannot be justified by any natural necessity. And this is indeed something which the very diversity of languages testifies to. Onomatopoeia, which some people have tried to interpret as being the basis of an original, clearly *motivated*, pre-Babel language, plays only a very marginal role in the lexicon:

> Bow-wow, says the dog,
> Mew, mew, says the cat,
> Grunt, grunt goes the hog,
> And squeak, goes the rat.
> Tu-whu, says the owl,
> Caw, caw, says the crow,
> Quack, quack, says the duck,
> And what cuckoos say you know.

Further, onomatopoeia is itself governed by the phonological constraints peculiar to each language: a British cockerel may go *cock-a-doodle-doo*, but a French one goes *cocorico* and a German one *kikiriki*!

There is a social corollary to the arbitrary nature of the sign: the assumption that there is agreement between speakers of the same language.

> The word 'arbitrary' [notes Saussure] should not convey the idea that the signifier depends on the choice of the speaking subject. . . . It is not within the power of the individual to change anything in a sign once it has been established within a linguistic group.[1]

By establishing his own conventions and refusing to conform to the consensus which brings speakers of the same language together in one linguistic community, Lewis Carroll's Humpty Dumpty is therefore undermining the very foundations of communication:

> 'I don't know what you mean by "glory",' Alice said.
> Humpty Dumpty smiled contemptuously. 'Of course you don't—till I tell you. I meant "there's a nice knock-down argument for you!" '
> 'But "glory" doesn't mean "a nice knock-down argument",' Alice objected.
> 'When *I* use a word,' Humpty Dumpty said, in a rather scornful tone, 'it means just what I choose it to mean—neither more nor less.'
> 'The question is,' said Alice, 'whether you *can* make words mean so many different things.'
> 'The question is,' said Humpty Dumpty, 'which is to be master—that's all'. (163)

Arbitrary, therefore, has the sense of 'conventional', 'relying on collective agreement'. However, we should note that not all codes can be defined exclusively in terms of the arbitrary. The Highway Code—to take just one example—which rests on the consensus of its users, is non-arbitrary in part since some of its signs are really ideograms: the one for a humpbacked bridge, for instance. Such things as airport signs are also, to a large extent, iconic.

Sign and Symbol

Émile Benveniste (1966) was later to criticize Saussure's concept, showing that the link between the two sides of the sign is in fact a *necessary* link—though unmotivated—precisely because the sign has no existence outside that link. What is strictly *arbitrary*, that is *non-necessary*, is the link between language and the world, between words and the reality designated, between a sign and its referent. This is the very link which speakers, quite innocently and with impeccable logic, attempt to justify and rationalize since, from their

---

[1] All Saussure quotations are from his posthumous *Cours de linguistique générale* published in Geneva in 1915.

point of view, language is what structures reality. A striking example is the division in many languages between *masculine* and *feminine* nouns, a division which is often interpreted as natural and deriving, metaphorically, from the male/female distinction affecting animate nouns.[2] Some objects or concepts, influenced by a quite arbitrary grammatical gender, are thus conceived of as essentially male or female. But the symbolic values derived from gender can be contradictory across cultures. Thus in French, *la lune* ('the moon') is a female entity as opposed to *le soleil* (the sun) but these values are reversed in German, which has *der Mond* and *die Sonne*. Death is represented as a male being in the North of Europe because of its gender in the Germanic languages and as a woman in the mythologies of Romance-speaking countries.

This last point brings us to the realization that it is essential to distinguish clearly between two quite different orders of meaning: sign and symbol. The latter, contrary to the sign, *is* motivated. In order to create a symbol, that is, one must be able to establish a necessary and justifiable link between symbolizer and symbolized. Any sign, or indeed any word, can symbolize another. Metaphor, itself, is a type of symbol formed within the system of signs constituted by language. 'Symbolization', writes Todorov (1977), 'is infinite, since anything which is symboli*zed* can, in turn, become a symbol*izer*, and so on in a never-ending chain of meaning.'

The extensions which can be given to the core meaning of a word are invariably motivated. The 'leg' of a table, for example, or 'arm' of a chair, evoke the human leg and arm (the literal meaning), the wing of an aeroplane evokes a bird's wing and so on. But these relationships are always established *within* language and take as read a *preliminary* categorization which, by contrast, is *not* motivated. I return to this topic in Chapter 12.

The creation of new words—neologisms—is also clearly motivated. For even though the basis of natural languages is essentially arbitrary, signs within them are linked by analogical and associative relationships. Thus the names of jobs or 'agents', for example, are all formed according to the same model (baker, draper, spinner, writer). And this applies to any new verb root. At the same time words are organized in series of *associative* terms or word 'families', sharing the same root morpheme.

So-called 'folk' etymologies, that is the meanings which speakers assign to unknown or invented words (cf. Chapter 5), proceed precisely from this system-internal motivation. What can *syntax* be if not 'a tax on sin'? And a *briefcase* is obviously 'a case for keeping your briefs in'. One takes a word and then finds a subsequent justification or semantic motivation for it. The point about this is that meaninglessness is something which drives the poor old signifier crazy! Any and every word positively craves to have a meaning

[2] Yaguello (1978).

assigned to it. In the well-known dictionary game, 'Call My Bluff' or 'Daffy Definitions', which consists of suggesting plausible definitions for words unknown to any of the players, it is precisely this capacity to imagine meaning—based on analogy- which is brought into play.

To return to Alice, when she hears the poem *Jabberwocky*, whose grammatical structure is clearly English, but whose vocabulary is largely invented, she comments: 'Somehow it seems to fill my head with ideas—only I don't exactly know what they are!' (118). Humpty Dumpty's subsequent explanation of the poem (an additional source of humour, since it does not correspond to the explanation given elsewhere by Carroll himself) exactly follows the rules of *Call My Bluff*.

Two quite different types of phenomena can be used in the interpretation of unknown or invented words. To take the case of Humpty first, a connection is established between an unknown or invented term, on the one hand, and, on the other, a word—and therefore a meaning—which actually exists in the language. The association of sounds in the unknown word with those in a known word sets up an association of *meaning*—an association which therefore operates wholly within the language—and for which Humpty offers a careful, rational explanation:

This sounded very hopeful, so Alice repeated the first verse:—

> ' 'Twas brillig, and the slithy toves
> 'Did gyre and gimble in the wabe:
> All mimsy were the borogroves,
> And the mome raths outgrabe.'

'That's enough to begin with,' Humpty Dumpty interrupted: 'there's plenty of hard words there. "*Brillig*" means four o'clock in the afternoon—the time you begin *broiling* things for dinner.'

'That'll do very well,' said Alice: 'and "*slithy*"?'

'Well, "*slithy*" means "lithe" and "slimy". "Lithe" is the same as "active". You see it's like a portmanteau—there are two meanings packed up into one word.'

'I see it now,' Alice remarked thoughtfully: 'and what are "*toves*"?'

'Well "*toves*" are something like badgers—they're something like lizards—and they're something like corkscrews.'

'They must be very curious-looking creatures.'

'They are that,' said Humpty Dumpty; 'also they make their nests under sun-dials—and also they live on cheese.'

'And what's to "*gyre*" and to "*gimble*"?'

'To "*gyre*" is to go round and round like a gyroscope. To "*gimble*" is to make holes like a gimblet.'

'And "*the wabe*" is the grass-plot round the sun-dial, I suppose?' said Alice, surprised at her own ingenuity.

'Of course it is. It's called "*wabe*", you know, because it goes a long way before it, and a long way behind it—'

'And a long way beyond it on each side,' Alice added.

'Exactly so. Well then, "*mimsy*" is "flimsy and miserable" (there's another port-manteau for you). And a "*borogrove*" is a thin, shabby-looking bird with its feathers sticking out all round—something like a live mop.'

'And then "*mome raths*"?' said Alice. 'I'm afraid I'm giving you a great deal of trouble.'

'Well, a "*rath*" is a sort of green pig: but "*mome*" I'm not certain about. I think it's short for "from home"—meaning that they'd lost their way, you know.'

'And what does "*outgrabe*" mean?'

'Well, "*outgribing*" is something between bellowing and whistling, with a kind of sneeze in the middle: however, you'll hear it done, maybe—down in the wood yon-der—and, when you've once heard it, you'll be quite content.' (164-6)

Sound Symbolism

To Humpty's crafty explanations must now be added another type of sym-bolism inherent to sound itself and perhaps universal, whose precise nature Jespersen, Sapir, and Jakobson, among others, have tried to define.

The close link [writes Jakobson[3]] between the sounds and the meanings of a word makes speakers want to complete this external relationship [that is an unmotivated association between a signifier and a signified] by an internal relationship, to treat what is merely contiguous as though it were similar, by way of some basic image. . . . For example, the opposition between high and low pitched phonemes can sug-gest an image of bright versus dark, pointed as opposed to rounded, thin versus fat, light versus heavy, and so on.

Or again, when presented with two unknown words—*mil* and *mal*—and told that one means 'large table' and the other 'small table', there is a very good chance indeed that *mal* will be associated with the idea of bigness and *mil* with smallness—Sapir, in fact, demonstrated this in an experiment. This is prompted, unconsciously of course, by the degree of openness of the vow-els (/i/ is closed, /a/ is open). Similarly, in another experiment (carried out by Köhler) when asked to assign the names *maluma* and *takete* to the two shapes in Figure 8.1, *maluma* is invariably associated with the cloud shape and *takete* with the star. Indeed, the back vowels (/u/, /o/, /a/) are perceived as dark, round, low-pitched and the front vowels (/i/, /e/) as light, pointed, and high-pitched: compare the transcription of a low-pitched male laugh—ha, ha—and a high-pitched feminine, or childish one—tee, hee. Other associations apply here, too. 'Closed' sounds are often interpreted as distin-guished, for example, while open sounds are considered vulgar.

Such associations, it would seem, are universal. Among the words which different languages use to distinguish between different kinds of noise—these

---

[3] [1942] 1976: 118 in the original French edition.

FIG. 8.1. Shapes associated with maluma and takete

are often onomatopoeic—the words which designate harsh or sudden noises very often begin with stops, that is plosives (p/b, t/d, k/g). The air suddenly escapes from the mouth all in one go: *ding, dong*; *bing, bang*; *crash*; *crunch*; *plop*. Strip cartoons abound in examples of such words. The words for progressive or continuous sounds, on the other hand, tend to begin with fricatives, that is continuants. Air is released gradually as in /s/ and /z/ or /ʃ/ and /ʒ/ or /f/ and /v/ as in *hiss, buzz, sizzle, swish, zip, zap, hush, shush*, and so on.

Finally, all languages contain so-called *ideophones*, that is stable associations between groups of sounds and ideas. In English, for example, *gl-* can be found at the beginning of a large group of words, all of which have something to do with light—*glare, gleam, glint, glisten, glow*—although it is impossible to justify this association. Moreover, on this occasion, it is not a universal one.

Associations between sound and meaning are peripheral in language systems as such, although they do play a role in poetry. Jakobson[4] reminds us that the symbolist poet, Stéphane Mallarmé (1842–1898), lamented the disharmony between the sound and the meaning in the words 'jour' and 'nuit' in his native French, with a dark (/u/) and clear (/i/) vowel, respectively. By way of contrast, in Russian the word for 'day' (*d'en'*) contains a high-pitched sound which is in opposition to a low-pitched sound in the word for 'night' (*noc'*).

The subject of sound symbolism, of course, raises the whole question of the value of imitative harmony in poetry and implicates such standard techniques as *assonance* (the repetition of vowels) or *alliteration* as in the immortal 'murmuring of innumerable bees', or the more pedestrian

> Large lively ladies leap in lyrical elation,
> Lick their lips and laugh aloud and that's alliteration!

Pope gave as a precept to poets that 'the sound must seem an echo of the sense'. But according to the American poet Gertrude Stein (1874–1946) 'Language, real language, does not imitate sounds, or colours, or emotions, it is intellectual recreation'. This is a point also taken up by Stein's contemporary, Paul Valéry (1871–1945) in his *Rhumbs*, where he writes:

The power of verse lies in the indefinable harmony between what it says and what it is. 'Indefinable' is part of the definition. This harmony must not be definable. If it is, it is imitative harmony and this is not good. The essence of verse lies in the impossibility of defining the relationship, combined with the impossibility of denying its existence. *A poem is a prolonged hesitation between sound and sense.* (emphasis mine)

Poetry, like music, we are invited to conclude, should evoke rather than imitate.

---

[4] [1942] 1976, 119 and [1960] 1987: 88.

9 The Incredible Lightness of Meaning
Sense and Nonsense

Take care of the sense and the sounds will take care of themselves.

(Lewis Carroll)

[Linguists] have tried everything to avoid meaning, ignore it or do away with it. Try as they might, meaning is still there at the heart of language, like a Medusa, petrifying those who look at it.

(Émile Benveniste)[1]

Meaning, strange as it may seem, was for a long time excluded from linguistics, especially by the followers of Saussure: functionalists, distributionalists, and structuralists. Roman Jakobson, in what is almost a caricature, tells the story of a comparative philologist who, after spending years deciphering an ancient manuscript was quite unable to call to mind its contents, since he had not even noticed them.

For Saussure the object of linguistics is the analysis of the linguistic units brought to light by segmentation and substitution (see above, Chapter 4). Having shown, and this is a major contribution, that linguistic units are organized as systems or structures, he is happy to leave it at that. But the question of the overall meaning of an utterance, requiring us to take into account the context and speech situation—where social and psychological factors come into play—does not arise.

Words, out of context, are signs uniting a signifier and a signified, but they have no *reference*: they are merely entries in the dictionary. An utterance, by contrast, has both meaning and reference: a meaning which is produced by the relationship the grammatical structure establishes between the signs and a reference which results from the relationship of the sentence uttered to a given situation, real or imaginary. For speakers, within the situation of utterance, meaning and reference are brought together, giving rise to *interpretation*. I return to this point in Chapter 11. But for the time being, we need to recognize a different level of meaning—found above all in poetry—which is independent of reference.

The reader of this chapter would not find much of the discussion which follows in conventional introductions to linguistics, since these tend to

---

[1] Benveniste (1974: 126).

concentrate on meaning in everyday language. In considering poetic uses we are able to explore hidden aspects of language and communication which are vividly highlighted in poetry and only dimly present in ordinary prose. In the words of Roman Jakobson, 'Poetics deals with problems of verbal structure. . . . Since linguistics is the global science of verbal structure, poetics may be regarded as an integral part of linguistics.'[2]

From Sounds to Utterances: The Construction of Meaning

From sounds to words and from words to utterances, each level plays a part in the construction of poetic meaning. Pure sound, as we have seen, produces evocative or symbolic meaning. At a higher level, in both mundane and poetic language, grammatical organization itself is meaningful. Alice, on hearing the nonsense poem *Jabberwocky*, says 'Somehow it seems to fill my head with ideas—only I don't exactly know what they are!', and adds, deriving an interpretation from the grammatical structure 'However, *somebody* killed *something*: that's clear at any rate' (118). Where proverbs, slogans and aphorisms are concerned, the 'tune' (that is, the phonic, rhythmic and syntactic structure) is just as important as the 'lyrics' (the words). The majority of Carroll's nonsense poems are corruptions of poems—for the most part very serious ones—well known to his Victorian public. Thus, the poem by Isaac Watts:

> How doth the little busy bee
> Improve each shining hour
> And gather honey all the day
> From every opening flower

becomes

> How doth the little crocodile
> Improve his shining tail
> And pour the waters of the Nile
> On every golden scale

Or again:

> Twinkle twinkle little bat
> How I wonder what you're at
> Up above the world you fly
> Like a tea-tray in the sky

[2] [1960] 1987: 63.

recited by the Mad Hatter (57), is a parody of Jane Taylor's famous poem:

> Twinkle twinkle little star
> How I wonder what you are
> Up above the world so high
> Like a diamond in the sky

(which also inspired the Beatles' song *Lucy in the Sky with Diamonds*).

In these cases, therefore, behind the nonsense is sense: the comic effect derives from the parody. Proverbs, with their grammatical, semantic, and rhythmic parallelism, lend themselves to parody particularly well, as in: 'Take care of the sense and the sounds will take care of themselves.' For speakers to interpret and enjoy such corruptions, they need to share the same frame of reference, i.e. be members of the same culture.

A more subtle analysis is required for a line which suggested itself to the French mathematician, François Le Lionnais, during a visit to a zoo: 'un singe de beauté est un jouet pour l'hiver.' A literal translation is of little use to us here—'a beautiful monkey is a toy for winter'?! What Le Lionnais has translated is the phonetic and rhythmic features of his original, John Keats's 'a thing of beauty is a joy forever'. The semantics of his new sentence bear a paronymic, almost surrealist relationship to the line from *Endymion*.

Now consider this text:

In the comment, Slander created the candle and the compost. Now, the compost was formless and empty, the content was over the surfer of the deep-sea diver and the skiff of Slander was hovering over the astonishment.

And Slander said, 'Let there be a candle end'; and there was a candle end. And Slander saw that the candle end was good. And Slander separated the candle end from the content. Slander called the candle end Newspaper and the content Overnight stay.

It is hard for anyone familiar with the Bible, not to recognize this totally zany text as a corruption of Genesis 1: 1–5. It is produced by going through the following stages: look up a translation of each noun in an English–French dictionary, then take the next noun in the same dictionary and translate it back into English. The result seems to make no sense at all. And yet, it still has the syntax, phrasing and rhythm characteristic of the Bible. In short, we recognize the tune, even if we do not know the words. In spite of everything, some semblance of meaning is produced, however tenuous, which we must obviously distinguish from 'rational', i.e. referential meaning.

A variation on the above exercise, known as the $N + 7$ *process*, consists of replacing each noun from the text with the one which comes seven nouns further on in a monolingual dictionary. The choice of dictionary can be significant. The poorer and the more elementary the dictionary, the more the text produced will tend to sound prosaic and concrete. The more comprehensive the dictionary, the more rare and archaic words the text will contain: the effect, consequently, will be more poetic—rare or unknown words having greater evocative power. One could almost say that the more imprecise a word, the more virtual meaning it contains, the less redundant or predictable it is. This is the paradox of meaning: meaning which is common, well known, worn out, tells us less than the unknown which gives free rein to our imagination:

Unusual words (neologisms, corruptions, archaisms, etc.) have poetic value inasmuch as they stand apart from the common words of the language of communication by virtue of their phonic effect. Common words, as a result of their frequent use, are no longer perceived in all the detail of their phonic composition, but rather felt.[3]

This is why Alice, during her fall down the rabbit hole, repeats with such pleasure the words *longitude* and *latitude*, which she does not understand at all but which, for that very reason, bear the stamp of mystery and poetry:

'I wonder what Latitude or Longitude I've got to?' (Alice had not the slightest idea what Latitude was, or Longitude either, but she thought they were nice grand words to say.) (8)

We can underline the point by quoting Jakobson again:

The more common the association between sound and sense, the more readily it becomes a mechanical one. Whence the conservative character of everyday language . . . In poetry, the role of automatic association is reduced to a minimum.[4]

Rhyme, in poetry, accentuates the phenomenon of the *diffusion* of meaning.[5] By establishing a relationship between signifiers which are alike, poetry thereby suggests a resemblance between the *signifieds* and this represents a powerful contribution to the construction of the overall meaning of the poem.

Jakobson has also shown the extent to which the grammatical parallelism characteristic of poetic utterances has an influence on meaning, thereby emphasizing the existence of 'grammatical devices' opposed to and superimposed upon 'stylistic devices'.[6] Indeed, grammatical parallelism institutes a 'coupling' of meaning, a process found notably in Biblical poetry:

> May those who curse you be cursed
> And those who bless you be blessed
>
> (Genesis, 27: 29)

> Out of the eater, something to eat;
> out of the strong, something sweet
>
> (Judges, 14: 14)

---

[3] 'Prague Linguistics Circle', in Faye and Robel (1969: 38).
[4] Jakobson ([1921] 1973: 20).   [5] Jakobson ([1961] 1973: 225).   [6] Ibid. 227.

In my distress I called to the Lord;
I called out to my God.
From his temple he heard my voice;
my cry came unto his ears

> (Samuel, 22: 7)

For he wounds, but he also binds up;
he injures, but his hands also heal

> (Job, 5: 18)

What is twisted cannot be straightened;
what is lacking cannot be counted . . .
For with much wisdom comes much sorrow;
the more knowledge, the more grief

> (Ecclesiastes, 1: 15–18)

The same process is also found in the ritual poetry of the oral traditions of numerous peoples.

Ritual language is oral poetry based on a binary system of meaning which requires the coupling of fixed elements to produce formulas and verse: this is a particular instance of the phenomenon of canonical repetition, whose widespread use in oral traditions throughout the world is only just starting to be studied.[7]

Poetic parallelism may be linked to the essentially binary rhythm which animates humankind: hence the universality of the practice. Humankind is bilateral, with a consequent interaction between gestures and words: 'Beneath the oral gesture lies the overall gesture of bilateral anthropos'.[8] It is this same binary oscillation that we find in nursery rhymes and proverbs: 'like father, like son'; 'all's well that ends well'; 'first come, first served'; 'more haste, less speed'; 'what goes up, must come down'; 'once a thief, always a thief' and so on. This kind of formulation—which can be reduced to two main types, opposition and comparison—makes a clear contribution to the meaning.

But meaning is not evenly spread through an utterance. Within the framework of OULIPO, Raymond Queneau and Jacques Bens carried out two experiments in the reduction of utterances which enabled them to determine which parts were most heavily loaded with meaning, or the least redundant and, then, to establish a hierarchy of grammatical classes according to the kind of meaning produced. Every speaker can somehow sense that nouns, verbs, adjectives, and adverbs are not equally important. The OULIPO experiment enables us to clarify this intuition by drawing up lists using texts in prose or verse. If we remove, in turn, nouns, adjectives, verbs and adverbs from context, we notice that only the first list retains a semblance

---

[7] Cf. Fox (1974).   [8] Jousse (1978: 95).

of meaning, the others producing fairly incoherent lists: the point is illustrated below, in relation to the nouns in the first verse of John Keats's 'Ode
to a Nightingale':

> My *heart* aches, and a drowsy *numbness* pains
>   My *sense*, as though of *hemlock* I had drunk,
> Or emptied some dull *opiate* to the *drains*
>   One *minute* past, and Lethe-wards had sunk:
> 'Tis not through *envy* of thy happy *lot*,
>   But being too happy in thine *happiness*,—
> That thou, light-winged Dryad of the *trees*,
>   In some melodious *plot*
> Of *beechen* green, and *shadows* numberless,
>   Singest of *summer* in full-throated *ease*.

This yields the following list, which, if read with feeling, retains some of the
evocative power of the original:

*heart, numbness, sense, hemlock, opiate, drains, minute, envy, lot, happiness, trees, plot,
beechen, shadows, summer, ease.*

If we had to include in our hierarchy the structure words (those that cannot stand alone: prepositions, conjunctions, articles, and particles) we
would, of course, find them right at the bottom of the scale of significance.
The great American poet and novelist, Gertrude Stein, who spent her life
reshaping language, breaking it up and then restructuring it, understood
this hierarchy very well, only *she* reversed it, drawing from it poetic effects
diametrically opposed to what we would expect. Above all, she detested
nouns and adjectives, was a little more indulgent towards verbs and
adverbs, had immense esteem for articles and conjunctions and was pas-
sionate about prepositions. She hated, indeed, everything which was too
directly referential, whence the impossibility, for Stein, of deriving poetic
effects from nouns—'which, unfortunately, so very, very unfortunately, are
the names of things'—or from adjectives, which are used to qualify those
things: whereas structure words are words which work, which do something and are not content to supply silly names. Such was Gertrude Stein
and the captivating method in her madness! By reducing language to its
redundant part, she was attempting—paradoxically—to renew its poetic
and semantic potential. No doubt she had little use for telegrams.

The Power of the Word: Linguistic Meaning in Rituals

Meaning is also closely linked to the functions brought into play within the
utterance. In rituals of every kind—magic, religious, or even ludic—the
formulas used, while they may be devoid of referential value, are rich in

significance: but a significance which owes nothing to an analysis of the parts of the utterance.[9] This is particularly true with nursery rhymes, other simple verse, and tangle talk or nonsense rigmaroles, which children use at play in ritualized games which combine gestures with words in an unchanging scenario. For example:

> Round and round the garden, like a teddy bear
> This little piggy went to market, this little piggy stayed home
> Ha ha ha hi hi hi, can't catch me for a toffee tree

Comptines or 'counting rhymes' are used quite literally to count the number of participants in a game and to assign different roles: 'one potato, two potato, three potato, four', 'ip dip sky blue', or 'eeny meeny miney mo'. Actually, with counting rhymes we enter the realm of 'Nonsense', a genre, of course, in which Lewis Carroll and Edward Lear excelled. But, as we saw in connection with *Jabberwocky*, non-sense is a long way from the *absence* of sense.

Sense, Nonsense and Reference

In poetry, as in ritual, everything invites us to make a distinction between sense and reference. What distinguishes the referential from the non-referential, for André Breton, is that in poetry meaning is unpremeditated. In surrealist metaphors and images, meaning bursts forth after the event, from associations which are random, not tediously contrived, since the poet has no referential aim in mind.

The meaning which we recognize *a posteriori*, often originating in nonsense or the violation of common sense, is similarly in evidence during a psychedelic trip: as evoked (some say), for example, in the Beatles' *Lucy in the Sky with Diamonds*:

> Follow her down to a bridge by a fountain
> Where rocking horse people eat marshmallow pies
> Everyone smiles as you drift past the flowers
> That grow so incredibly high

Breton, indeed, had already compared the effects of surrealism with those of hashish: a comparison all smokers of pot will recognize. Its effects are noticeable, above all, in the smoker's speech, which is largely devoid of premeditation and the intention to communicate. The speech of someone who is hallucinating is not the same as pathological speech, although they share certain features. What characterizes speech during hallucination is the intensity of the meaning for the speaker, even if that meaning is inaccessible to

---

[9] Cf. Baudrillard (1980: 118).

others: it is anything but the absence of meaning. Few are better placed to speak of this, perhaps, than the Franco-Belgian poet Henri Michaux (1899-1984), who explored its every aspect in *Connaissance par les gouffres* (1961). He emphasizes 'the tendency to neologism in people who had never before displayed it . . . a tendency to form by agglutination the new words they require'. We can even wonder if Alice's own experiments with mushrooms—which make her now bigger, now smaller—are not of a hallucinogenic nature:[10] this would explain her loss of identity and the nasty tricks her memory plays on her when, talking to the Caterpillar, she makes a vain attempt to recite poetry.

Paradoxically for common sense, therefore, it would seem that meaning may exist independently of the speaker's intention and the latter's assumed reference and communicative aim and that—conversely—nonsense can also result from the speaker's intention. As we have seen, nonsense is simply another form of sense, which is perverse, polymorphic. Where do its limits lie? At what point does sense exhaust itself?

From Word to Sound: The Destruction of Meaning

'Where words end, music begins'

(Haydn)

Meaning is vulnerable. We saw earlier how Verlaine defined poetry as a 'prolonged hesitation between sound and meaning'. A gentle nudge is enough to destroy this delicate balance. By giving priority to pure sound, we leave the way open to meaninglessness, the absence of meaning, as distinct from nonsense. The link between signifier and signified is a vulnerable one. It can be lost, just as it can be created.

Roman Jakobson observed of the futurist Victor Khlebnikov (1885-1922), that:

Meaning is muffled and euphonic structure is autonomous. We are only a short step from arbitrary language. . . . Poetic language, ultimately, tends towards purely phonetic words . . . a transmental discourse.[11]

And that short step is taken, the limit is reached when

Words . . . no longer have any designs on reality, lose their internal and, finally, their external shape.[12]

---

[10] A thesis by Thomas Fensch (*Lewis Carroll, The First Acid Head*) presents Alice's adventures as a work of psychedelic inspiration: the heroine attaches great importance to the intake of certain substances—liquids, cakes, *mushrooms*. Each time these result in mental and physical transformations.

[11] Jakobson ([1921] 1973: 24).   [12] Ibid.

As Raymond Queneau put it, with reference to Stéphane Mallarmé, what we have here is a 'Mallarmachine for creating a vacuum'. The Russian linguist Evgueni Polivanov, in distinguishing between poetry and prose, uses as his criterion the absolute primacy of phonetic organization over semantic organization. Poetry, above all, should play with sound as substance: 'It is not just the nature of a semantic content which is of no importance, but its very presence.'[13]

The organization of autonomous sounds is characteristic of the Russian formalists, in what they were to call the zaoum, literally the 'transmental'. In the zaoum (at least the ideal *zaoum* with no meaningful words), writes Polivanov:

all the author's creative energy and the attention of the receiver (reader or listener) are concentrated on the formal (phonic) aspects of the discourse: in other words, on the play of such and such a repetition, without being distracted by semantic representations.[14]

The same tendency to desemanticization can be found in France in movements like Dadaism or Lettrism. The German painter and musician, Kurt Schwitters (1887–1948), illustrated this trend in his *Ursonate*, composed of the repetition and chanting of strings of phonemes which are deliberately stripped of linguistic meaning.

Kurt Schwitters   KEY TO READING SOUND POEMS

As the English language is very difficult for exact sounds, I choose the simpler sounds of the German language. A e i o u are simple sounds, not ou, or ju, as o and u are in English.

And I go back to simple consonants. If consonants may be expressed by two others, I don't use them; for example, instead of z in German sounds, I say ts. If two vowels are written, that means a longer sound than one. If two vowels are to be spoken as two, I separate them. Aa is a long a, a a are two a.

Consonants are without sound; if they are to be sounded, the vowel of the sound is to be written: b be bö bee.

If consonants such as b p d t g h follow one another, they are to be spoken bbb as three single b.

If any of f h l j m n r s w ch sch (sh) follow one another, they are not to be spoken separately, but as one long consonant. e q v x y z are not used. W is not double u as in English, but like the English v.

Big letters are like small, they only mark a better separation. The English vowels a, i are printed ä, ei; the French u—ü; the Norwegian ø—ö.

Source: Raoul Hausmann and Kurt Schwitters, *PIN* (London: Gaber bocchus Press, 1962), 52.

---

[13] Polivanov ([1929] 1970).   [14] Ibid.

1922–1932	Exerpt from *Ursonate*	

einleitung:

Fümms bö wö tää zää Uu,   I
      pögriff,
        kwii Ee.

Ooooooooooooooooooooooooooooooooooo,   6

  dll rrrrrr beeeee bö,   (A)   5
  dll rrrrrr beeeee bö fümms bö,
    rrrrrr beeeee bö fümms bö wö,
      beeeee bö fümms bö wö tää,
        bö fümms bö wö tää zää,
          fümms bö wö tää zää Uu:

erster teil:

thema 1:
Fümms bö wö tää zää Uu,   I
      pögriff,
        kwii Ee.

thema 2:
Dedesnn nn rrrrrr,   2
      Ii Ee,
        mpiff tillff too,
          tillll,
            Jüü Kaa? (*gesungen*)

thema 3:
Rinnzekete bee bee nnz krr müü?   3
        ziiuu ennze, ziiuu rinnzkrrmüü,

  rakete bee bee.   3a

thema 4:
Rrummpff tillff toooo?   4

(Kurt Schwitters, *Ursonate*)

By this stage, language no longer shows the slightest trace of communicative value. Playing with words is nothing more than playing with *empty forms*. Indeed, this is play in its purest form, from which all aims are excluded. At this point, we have crossed the threshold of communication. We could argue that if we push too far, this process takes us beyond poetry: for even poetry has to retain *some* communicative potential, however small. Poetry, after all, justifies its existence by being, among other things, a form of communion between beings. 'Sound poetry is only of interest to the extent that it constitutes the very edge of poetic experience (of language): we should be able to reach that limit, but we should not do so in isolation.'[15]

'Where words end,' said Haydn, 'music begins.' The repetition of an isolated word, as all of us have noticed at some time or another, empties it of its meaning. We feel something approaching anxiety when—fortunately only for a fleeting moment—the meaning of the word is lost to us. It is suspended there, in our memory, reduced to a pure sound substance. Similarly, if I stare at the last word I wrote, or if I start covering an entire page with the same word, gradually it becomes alien to me, weird, incomprehensible, almost grotesque. It is nothing more than a drawing on a sheet of paper.

Contemporary music, with its characteristic repetitions, turns this into a technique. The repetition of unconnected words transforms them into pure sound substance, into music for which the instrument is the human voice. Synthetic or electro-acoustic music proceeds by dividing, editing, and superimposing (sometimes in the form of a canon) banal, pre-recorded messages. The result is a verbal music emptied of all linguistic value. We could mention here the *Suite for Edgar Poe* by Guy Reibel, or *Vox Vocis* by Ivo Malec, or again, Toru Takemitsu's variations on the word *aï*, which is Japanese for 'love'. It is also worth noting that classical music produces similar effects: listen, for example, to the 'Ave' in Schubert's *Stabat Mater*. The written word lends itself to a similar treatment as shown by graphic poetry or calligrammes, which privilege the outlines or forms of words to the detriment of meaning, or which, on the contrary, from that form produce a new meaning.

Easter wings

Lord, who createdst man in wealth and store,
Though foolishly he lost the same,
Decaying more and more,
Till he became
Most poore: 5
With thee
O let me rise
As larks, harmoniously,
And sing this day thy victories:
Then shall the fall further the flight in me.   10

My tender age in sorrow did beginne:
And still with sicknesses and shame
Thou didst so punish sinne,
That I became
Most thinne.   15

[15] Todorov (1972).

> With thee
> Let me combine
> And feel this day thy victorie:
> For, if I imp my wing on thine,
> Affliction shall advance the flight in me.   20
>
> (George Herbert, 'Easter Wings')

The philosopher Jean Baudrillard points out that ritual formulas, chanted to the point of intoxication, have the same aim:

Words and gestures are emptied of their meaning by endless repetition and chanting: tire meaning, wear it out, extenuate it, so as to free the seductive purity of the zero signifier, the empty term—such is the strength of ritual magic and incantation.[16]

A religious trance is always accompanied by these vocal manifestations, which blur the boundaries between the mystical, the hallucinatory, and the pathological.

There is much interesting work waiting to be done about the semantic bleaching of the word in song: in opera especially. Musicians tend towards vocal music because they are tempted by that which is intelligible. The spoken word is rational, whereas music is not and the human voice is where music and the spoken word meet. In opera, spoken word and music are overlaid, but the spoken message is dissolved in the musical one (we have little difficulty in listening to an opera in a foreign language), indeed, itself becomes music. The role of recitative is simply to ensure that the narrative is understood: it ensures the transition between singing, which hinders action and speaking, which moves it forward. When singers vocalize, therefore, they are in a sense returning to the infantile stage of babbling, an activity which has no aim other than the production of sound per se, for pleasure. 'When we exit language, we exit history and so approach myth, childhood and therefore the childhood of humanity—whence an analogy between music and myth.'[17]

---

[16] Baudrillard (1980).   [17] Oriano (1980).

The House that Jack Built

Competence and Performance

Words are merely the reflection of what we say. The linguist's job is to find an intermediate mirror—a mirror-language. If my speech is reflected in your language, it means we are both speaking the same one. The loss of any reflection can make us stammer or strike us dumb.

(anon. *M.O. et Camées*)

Recursiveness: The Non-Finiteness of Language

'Never imagine yourself not to be otherwise than what it might appear to others that what you were or might have been was not otherwise than what you had been would have appeared to them to be otherwise', [said the Duchess.] 'I think I should understand that better,' said Alice very politely, 'if I had it written down: but I can't quite follow it as you say it.' 'That's nothing to what I could say if I chose,' the Duchess replied in a pleased tone.
'Pray don't trouble yourself to say it any longer than that,' said Alice. (72)

What ability is it that the Duchess is so proud of? Many of us have, at some point, found ourselves standing between two mirrors and been unsettled by the infinite regression of images produced. Or again, we may have seen on television, a presenter flanked by a monitor on whose screen he appears with, at his side, a monitor in which he appears with a monitor at his side, in which he appears with a monitor at his side, in which . . .

There is no particular reason why I should end the sentence at that point—aside, that is, from boring the reader half to death, or running out of paper! Indeed, the sentence is theoretically infinite. The only limit to the number of television screens we might count in the sequence of images my sentence describes, is the technical ability (or inability) of the first television screen to represent infinity, or our own inability to conceive of it.

In the same way, the limits to the length of any sentence are determined by psychological or cognitive, that is non-linguistic factors—short-term memory, the ability to process complex messages or make stylistic choices— all of which vary enormously between speakers.

There is a discrepancy, in consequence, between the *potential* within language and speakers' *actual* use of it. This is why Alice's reaction to the

Duchess is so significant. Alice might perhaps just manage to analyse and then understand the complex sentence which the Duchess reels off, if only she could write it down and take a little time to work her way through it.

When R. D. Laing—psychiatrist, social theorist, poet—writes the following, the majority of readers probably beg for mercy from around the third line on:

JILL I'm upset you are upset
JACK I'm not upset
JILL I'm upset that you're not upset that I'm upset you're upset
JACK I'm upset that you're upset that I'm not upset that you're upset that I'm upset, when I'm not.[1]

In a similar way 'I know you believe you understand what you think I said, but I'm not sure you realize that what you hear is not what I meant you to understand' soon becomes rather difficult to follow, even with the best will in the world. Or again, what spectator at the theatre could possibly keep up with the following story from Eugène Ionesco's *The Bald Prima Donna*?

THE FIREMAN. 'The Cold': My brother-in-law had, on his father's side, a first cousin, one of whose maternal uncles had a father-in-law whose paternal grandfather's second wife was a native whose brother had met, while on his travels, a girl whom he'd fallen for and with whom he had a son who married an intrepid pharmacist's wife who was none other than the daughter of an unknown quarter-master in the British merchant navy and whose adoptive father had an aunt who spoke fluent Spanish and who was perhaps one of the grandchildren of an engineer, who died young, himself the grandson of the owner of a vineyard, which produced a mediocre wine, but who had a distant cousin, a stay-at-home type, an adjutant, whose son had married a jolly pretty young lady, a divorcee, whose first husband was a sincere patriot who had instilled in one of his daughters the desire to make a fortune, who married a hunter who had known Rothschild and whose brother, having tried his hand at several jobs, married and had a daughter, whose great-grandfather, a scrawny man, wore glasses given to him by a cousin, brother-in-law of a Portuguese, illegitimate son of a miller, not too poor, whose foster brother had taken as his wife the daughter of a former country doctor, himself the foster brother of the son of a milkman, himself the illegitimate son of another country doctor, three times married, whose third wife . . .
MR MARTIN. I knew the third wife, unless I'm much mistaken. She used to eat chicken out of a wasp's nest.
THE FIREMAN. No. That wasn't the same woman.

Many more examples can be found in popular songs, rhymes, and ditties. Generations of English-speaking children have crossed the language barrier and grown up to the strains of 'je te plumerai la tête . . . et la tête, et les

---

[1] Laing, (1971: 21).

pieds etc.' even if they did not always understand what they were singing! 'The House that Jack Built' and 'I Know an Old Lady Who Swallowed a Fly' are two other examples in the same vein.

Although difficult to understand, all these utterances and others of their kind are perfectly well formed. All of them conform to the grammatical rules of the English language. And none of them violate any semantic rules. What all our examples here clearly demonstrate is that one of the essential characteristics of language is its capacity to produce utterances with a potentially infinite number of embedded or coordinated clauses. This property is known as *recursiveness*.[2] The simple juxtaposition or coordination of verbs, nouns, adjectives, adverbs, and groups of words *within* clauses, further contributes to this snowball effect: for example, 'he was handsome, rich, intelligent, friendly . . . '; or, 'they were all there—Andrew, David, George, Patrick . . . and the others'. The sentence can be defined, then, as a unit of discourse containing either a *single* clause (which can consist of any number of phrases of any length) or a *main* clause + any number of coordinate or subordinate clauses from one to infinity.

Language, with its finite number of sounds and words, selected and combined according to a finite number of rules, can give the impression of being—like chess[3]—a finite combinatorial structure. However vast the vocabulary or grammar rules of a given language, one might think that it ought to be possible, with the aid of a computer, to draw up a complete list of the sentences in the language, just as it is a theoretical possibility (at least for a computer program) to predict all the possible moves in a chess match.

And yet, this is not the case.

If—as we have seen—there is no limit to the *length* (and therefore complexity) of sentences, that is, no limit to the number of embedded or linked elements, it follows that there is no limit to the *number* of sentences which a language can generate. The most powerful computer in the world would never be able to count them all. Any sentence, as we have just seen, can 'snowball' indefinitely.

Noam Chomsky is not the first person to have noticed this apparently innocent principle, as our reading of the work of Lewis Carroll has shown, to say nothing of Ionesco's inextinguishable fireman. On the other hand,

---

[2] A number of literary works are based around the same principle of embedding. For example, *The Manuscript Found in Saragossa*, in which a man tells the story of a man who, in turn, is telling the story of a man who, in turn, is telling a story of a man who is telling a story . . . etc.

[3] Indeed, language has often been compared with chess. The *pieces* and the *rules* of chess can be likened to what Ferdinand de Saussure called *langue* (or *language system*), while a chess *match* would be analogous to Saussure's *parole* (or *speech*). And yet, unlike language, a chess match has no referent. Each chess piece may have a 'meaning' and a function, but the game refers only to itself.

Chomsky was the first to draw out the theoretical consequences of recursiveness in his famous work *Syntactic Structures*, published in 1957, in which he laid the groundwork of what was to become a dominant linguistic theory for the rest of the century.[4]

Competence and Performance

Linguistic *competence*, for Chomsky, is what enables every *native speaker* of a given language to create an *infinite* number of sentences from a *finite* number of units, using a finite set of rules. A speaker can spontaneously produce and understand an infinite number of sentences which s/he has never produced or heard before. Recursiveness, in other words, gives language a *creative* dimension. We shall see in later chapters how the imaginative use of words—wordplay, breaking the rules which govern word selection (notably in figures of speech), the invention of words, neologisms (popular or academic), in short everything which makes language live, develop, and explore its own limits (especially in poetry)—constitutes another form of creativity of which speakers are far more consciously aware.

But we are clearly talking about two quite different types of creativity. The first type, a consequence of recursive rules, is inherent within language and is part of the *linguistic competence* of any speaker of any language. The second type of creativity, however, belongs to *performance*, that is the *actualization* of competence by a given individual: as such it depends on the speaker. Competence, we might say, is *virtual*. Performance actualizes this virtual capacity which, by its very nature, is variable from one speaker to another. If we return for a moment to our comparison between language and a game, the game, in this instance, consists of constant reinvention. At the level of Saussure's *parole*, the game of language provides a non-stop stream of unexpected, never-before-heard language. Our comparison stops there, however, since the rules of the linguistic 'game' are internalized, unconscious, while the rules of real games are consciously acquired.

Chomsky vs. Saussure

The Chomskian opposition between *competence* and *performance* is reminiscent of but does not exactly coincide with the distinction, drawn half a century earlier by Saussure between *langue* and *parole*. For Saussure,

---

[4] Some would say a dogma, which is increasingly challenged today in many quarters, e.g. by the functionalists, cognitivists and sociolinguists.

langue exists within the collectivity as a set of impressions in each brain, rather like a dictionary, identical copies of which have been handed out to all the speakers. It is something, then, which is within every one of them, while at the same time being common to all of them, yet beyond its owner's control (my emphasis). *Parole* is the sum of what people say and includes: (a) the deliberate individual combinations of those speaking; (b) the equally deliberate physical production of sounds necessary to form these combinations.[5]

Langue, therefore, is *social* and serves to define a linguistic community, which is held to be homogeneous, as alluded to in the epigraph to this chapter ('If my speech is reflected in your language, it means we are speaking the same one'). *Parole*, on the other hand, is *individual* and Saussure elects not to concern himself with it.[6] None of which, of course, prevents individual deviations from *parole*, as soon as they acquire collective status, from having a retrospective effect on *langue*, which then enables the latter to develop. Set or lexicalized metaphors, for example, become part of the language system; *connotations*, which are by nature social, end up changing the nature of *denotation*, which is part of the framework of *langue*.

Thus far the difference between the two conceptual frameworks is only apparent. For Chomsky, however, creativity affects *both* competence (since it is a property of recursive rules) *and* performance (individual productions), whereas Saussure only sees creativity in *parole*, since, for him, the sometimes deviant utterance is a result of individual manipulation and does not reflect *langue*. He does not see the grammar internalized by the native speaker as a generative device. The sentence in Saussurean linguistics belongs to the realm of *discourse*, an idea emphasized by Benveniste:

The sentence is undefined creativity, limitless variety, it is the very lifeblood of language in action. From which we conclude that, with the sentence, we leave behind us the territory of *la langue* as a system of signs and enter a different world: the world of language as instrument of communication which is expressed through discourse.[7]

A further significant difference is that Chomsky postulates an underlying universal grammar, common to all human beings, which opens onto diversified surface grammars, under the action of syntactic transformations specific to each language. Chomskian competence then, over and above a language competence which can be broadly equated with the Saussurean concept, is a specific human, genetically-based competence-for-language.

---

[5] Saussure ([1915] 1968: 38), in the original French edition.

[6] Saussure uses a musical analogy to convey the significance of the discrepancy between *langue* and *parole*: a symphony, even when it contains a number of wrong notes, remains nonetheless intact as a virtual entity, which suggests that parole, subjected as it is to human manipulation, constitutes a devalued manifestation when compared with *langue* which, by implication,is an ideal. In the same way that music does not have to be played in order to exist, the existence of *langue* is independent of *parole*.

[7] 1966: 128-9.

And here we find a link with Descartes and the *Grammaire générale et raisonnée*,[8] a 'universal grammar', created in the seventeenth century by two scholars at the Abbey of Port-Royal in Paris.

It was *langue* which was earmarked by Saussure as the object of study for linguistics, considering as he did that *parole* was part of a different area of linguistics which he did not intend to tackle. This was to be a linguistics of the utterance, to which Saussure relegated everything which is closely linked to the context of speech, particularly meaning. 'By separating "langue" from "parole", we also separate at the same time (1) what is social from what is individual, (2) the essential from what is more or less incidental, even accidental.'[9]

Saussure's dichotomy, which was long taken as gospel, is open to criticism. His position, however rigorous, is weakened by a paradox. *Langue*, a social phenomenon, can only be observed through *parole* or individual expression. Yet *parole* is itself influenced by the social relationships which develop in every linguistic community and cannot be explained without reference to these. As early as the 1920s, a Russian philosopher, Mikhail Bakhtin (alias Volochinov), was critical of Saussure's vision which made of the linguistic sign an inflexible 'signal', with no account taken of the context of the utterance which, in the end, can alone give the sign its meaning. For Bakhtin (1929), words are the site of a constant struggle between modulations of meaning which vary according to who is speaking and what the situation is: consider, for example, a word like *democracy*. A word, for Bakhtin, is an arena where the class struggle is fought out.

Let us take up, once again, our analogy between language and play. The rules of a game can be compared to linguistic competence. But we now know that competence can be socially modified: it is no longer possible to defend Saussure's vision of *langue* as context-free. Quite clearly, the word 'social' did not have for Saussure the same meaning as it has for us today. For him, society was a homogeneous, harmonious whole, brought together by the same language system. But, as we know, society is divided, conflictual, unstable. By eliminating *parole* from his field of scientific study, Saussure effectively eliminated the speaker as a social being and reduced the variation in the use of language to mere individual differences which he took to be quite insignificant.

But neither can it be said that Chomsky, by reintroducing the idea of the speaker via the sentence, has really resolved this contradiction. For

[8] Port-Royal, a convent of Cistercian nuns originally based at Chevreuse, between Versailles and Rambouillet, became an important centre of intellectual opposition to Louis XIV's regime soon after being transferred to Paris in 1625. Published in 1660, the *Grammaire* of Arnauld and Lancelot was an application of Cartesian doctrine to the analysis of language.

[9] [1915] 1968: 30.

Chomsky's speaker is also an idealized, abstract being, cut off from both context of utterance and social background. In a much quoted passage he states:

Linguistic theory is concerned primarily with an *ideal listener-speaker*, in a *completely homogeneous speech-community*, who knows its language perfectly and is unaffected by such grammatically irrelevant conditions as memory limitations, distractions, shifts of attention and interest, and errors (random or characteristic) in applying his knowledge of the language in actual performance.[10] (emphasis mine)

The rules of the linguistic game are invariably played out in a social context, which superimposes another set of rules or constraints upon them. It becomes difficult to see how this can be dismissed as part of a merely individual parole or performance. Criticizing the Chomskian dichotomy, Dell Hymes (1972) uses a simile which I find both illuminating and amusing. Competence is like the garden of Eden, out of which the ideal speaker-listener is thrust into the fallen world of performance, as soon as s/he commits the sin of utterance. Redemption can only come from a redefinition of competence. To use language successfully and creatively we need a different kind of competence—communicative competence—and no account of language and language use is complete unless the role of communicative competence is considered. I return to this point in the last section of this chapter.

Accidents of Performance

But in addition to this sociolinguistic dimension of language use, we must make room for psychological parameters. The speaker is an individual driven by both conscious and *unconscious* motivations. Indeed, contrary to competence, which is an abstract construction, performance, the concrete use of language in speech, is at the mercy of the unconscious. Performance exhibits failures or accidents which cannot be put down to a weakness in competence. Language, as it were, can break down in a number of ways.

An emotionally disturbed speaker can *momentarily* lose the power of speech or produce incoherent, ungrammatical speech ('the loss of any reflection can make us stammer or strike us dumb'). This is what happens to poor Alice who, in the grip of a powerful emotion after her excessive growth, goes all to pieces and can no longer correctly form a comparative ('curiouser and curiouser'). What we have here is a deficiency in performance, not competence.

---

[10] Chomsky (1965: 3). Over the years, Chomsky's theory has gone through many different stages (the current version is called the *Minimalist program*) but his position over the speaker, as far as I know, has not varied.

The pathological symptoms of aphasics, whose language competence has been damaged, mirror the *accidents* of performance which we can observe in 'normal' subjects: slips of the tongue, verbal tics, words which are forgotten, inverted, confused, or deformed. Similarly, *deliberate* corruption of language (play on words, invented words, spoonerisms, portmanteau words) find their equivalents in the speech of aphasics (jargonophasia) and in glossolalia (speaking in tongues) when a subject is possessed, often under the influence of some mystical ecstasy, speaking an invented language which s/he cannot control.

Thus in a person suffering from some language disorder, it is competence which is affected. Accidents of performance (slips of the tongue, etc.) can be put right. A poetic frenzy and a pathological frenzy are separated by intention, although the dividing line is not always very clear (consider Artaud, Beckett, Blake, and Joyce). For a sick person, however, such symptoms are generally irreversible. I return to this topic in Chapter 11.

A child's 'mistakes' paradoxically reveal the existence of linguistic competence. For example the over-generalization of irregular past tense forms— such as *comed, goed*—are related to creativity and prove that the child has acquired the main mechanisms of language. As we have noted before, in children performance often lags behind competence: a child 'recognizes' correct statements before it is able to produce them.

Linguistic 'howlers' which a number of authors have collected, from school exercise books or letters to insurance companies, are often accidents of performance arising from lack of attention, or sometimes from the very real traps laid by ambiguous syntactic structures—'my grandad's just had all his teeth taken out and a new electric fire put in' (see Chapter 14)—but also from the difficulties inherent in producing written language (the causes of which are essentially social). This is why those 'in the know' laugh at howlers. Some speakers find it difficult to cope with 'long words', especially those that come from Latin or Greek: 'Speak English!' said the Eaglet. 'I don't know the meaning of half those long words, and, what's more, I don't believe you do either!' (45).

Confusing such words is the speciality of the character in *Joseph Andrews*, appropriately called 'Mrs Slipslop', who protests for example: 'Barbarous monster! how have I deserved that my passion should be resulted and treated with ironing?'. A similar character, Mrs Malaprop, is found in Sheridan's *The Rivals*:

MRS MALAPROP. Observe me Sir Anthony,—I would by no means wish a daughter of mine to be a progeny of learning; I don't think so much learning becomes a young woman; for instance—I would never let her meddle with Greek, or Hebrew, or Algebra, or Simony, or Fluxions, or Paradoxes, or such inflammarory branches of learning—neither would it be necessary for her to handle any of your mathematical, astronomical, diabolical instruments;—But, Sir Anthony, I would send her, at nine years old, to a boarding school, in order to learn a little ingenuity and artifice.—Then, Sir, she would have a supercilious knowledge in accounts;—and as she grew up, I would have her instructed in geometry, that she might know something of the contagious countries;—but above all, Sir Anthony, she would be mistress of orthodoxy, that she might not mis-spell, and mis-pronounce words so shamefully as girls usually do; and likewise that she might reprehend the true meaning of what she is saying.

(Act I, scene ii)

But here it is perhaps as much a matter of competence as of performance.

Language and the Unconscious

Slips of the tongue, spoonerisms, and portmanteau words, inasmuch as they reveal the unconscious, have been widely studied, particularly by Freud in his *Jokes and their Relation to the Unconscious* (1905) and *The Psychopathology of Everyday Life* (1901). I refer readers to these texts and would simply emphasize that the portmanteau word is a *condensation* and that, generally speaking, the slip of the tongue often reveals intentions which are diametrically opposed to those the speaker is attempting to express: hence the term 'Freudian slip'. A journalist spoke one day on the radio about the 'Security Council of the United States', whereas, of course, he meant to say 'of the United Nations', a Freudian slip if ever there was, when one thinks of the dominant role played by the United States in that organization. President Jacques Chirac of France made the same slip when making a speech about the role of the UN in the conflict in former Yugoslavia. Or witness the example of a French novelist who, when invited to take part in a famous literary and cultural programme called *Apostrophes*, was thrown into an excitable state and said to one of her friends 'guess who's going to be on *Catastrophes* with me', or the case of the lecturer in history who announced to his students that he was about to give them a 'hysterical scotch'.

Mistakes can arise, quite simply, through the fear of making a mistake. Many people who, contrary to Mrs Slipslop or Mrs Malaprop, do know the difference between, say, 'perpetrate' and 'perpetuate', or 'condone' and 'condole' or 'affect' and 'effect' confuse the two nonetheless, precisely because they are afraid of confusing them.

Polysemy and homophony, although part of *langue*, can equally serve to reveal the unconscious, when they appear in the speech of a patient under analysis. They are of cardinal importance for psychoanalysis in that they introduce into speech a double meaning, ambiguity, the unavowed and the unspeakable. We know how much importance Jacques Lacan and his followers attach to the unintended pun: the seemingly random but revealing convergence, that is, of two different signifieds in one signifier, as in the

French pairing *mer*/*mère* ('sea'/'mother'). It can often be difficult to tell the difference between a deliberate pun and an unintentional one and their role in psychoanalysis is perhaps open to criticism at times. Be that as it may, the convergence within the field of language activity of, on the one hand, Freudian slips and, on the other, deliberate wordplay forces us to question and to clarify both the Saussurean notion of *la langue* and the Chomskian one of 'competence'.

Criticizing an article published in 1910 by Freud, 'On the contradictory meanings of primitive words', Benveniste argues that if the unconscious is structured like a language, it is with *parole* that the symbolism of the unconscious should be compared and not with *langue*. The universal symbolism of the unconscious can be related to the universal features of language which, by transcending the supposedly neutral cultural system of *langue*, in fact reveal themselves in the *parole* of all peoples.

It is in style [that is, in speech] rather than *langue* that we would find a point of comparison with the properties Freud discerned as identifying the 'language' of dreams. Some striking analogies suggest themselves. The unconscious employs a genuine rhetoric which, like style, has its 'figures of speech' and the time-honoured list of tropes would provide an inventory appropriate for both levels of expression. On both sides can be found all the methods of substitution generated by taboos: euphemism, allusion, antiphrasis, paralipsis and litotes. The nature of the content will provoke the use of all kinds of metaphor, for the symbols of the unconscious derive both their meaning and their obscurity from metaphorical conversion. They also use what traditional rhetoric used to call metonymy (the container for the contained) and synecdoche (the part for the whole). And if the 'syntax' of sequences of symbols evokes a stylistic technique at all, it is ellipsis.[11]

And Benveniste again underlines the parallel with poetic creativity:

Certain poetic forms can resemble dreams, suggest the same kind of structure and introduce into normal forms of language the suspension of meaning that dreams project into our waking activity. It was in surrealist poetry which, according to Breton, Freud did not understand, that the latter might—paradoxically—have found something of what he was mistakenly looking for in organized language.

If we accept Benveniste's arguments, we are led to conclude that the unconscious is reflected in parole without being filtered by *langue*. Creative speech, conscious or unconscious, owes nothing to *langue*: a paradoxical situation when one bears in mind that, in Saussure's view, *parole* is but an actualization of *langue*.

By way of contrast, Jakobson, on a number of occasions, underlined that the mechanism of figures of speech (in particular metaphor and metonymy) corresponded to the two main organizing principles of language: selection (along the paradigmatic axis) and combination (along the syntagmatic axis),

[11] Benveniste (1966: 82–3).

the destructured language of aphasics being due to the loss of these structuring capacities.

Let us consider language as being what all humanity has in common—a genetically determined, though culturally developed ability for expression through an articulated code or sign system, endowed with universal characteristics such as double articulation, redundancy, recursiveness, ambiguity, dissymmetry, etc. It is clear, then, that the aptitude for using symbols (setting up symbolic relationships within a given language) and stylistic devices, for violating—playfully or poetically—the rules of language, for creatively exploiting ambiguity, in short everything which has been grouped together under the heading 'creative performance', conscious or unconscious, proceeds from the language ability. In a way the speaker is programmed for this. From the community into which the speaker is integrated, s/he receives a 'language system' with a set of 'instructions for use', but also a set of 'counter-instructions' (a set of *decon*structions?) the use of which is merely another way of demonstrating one's mastery of the instructions. Playing on an ambiguity, for example, *reaffirms* a distinction while pretending to be ignorant of it, for a comic effect is not achieved if one is not aware of the ambiguity. 'Jokes about language always include "the reminder of a certain linguistic knowledge" (negatively, in so far as it is violated).'[12]

Language in its Social Context: Communicative Competence

'Would you tell me, please,' said Alice, a little timidly . . . 'Speak when you're spoken to', interrupted the Queen of Hearts. (63)

The Queen represents Alice's governess, the person who is responsible for teaching Alice the Victorian rules of politeness. The Queen of Hearts's reproof brings painfully home to her the fact that it is not for children to initiate conversations with adults or strangers of a higher status. Alice uses the polite language and forms of address which are considered proper for a 7-year-old, middle-class girl in the nineteenth century. Each time she speaks to a new character she is always concerned to select from her code what seems to her to be the appropriate forms of address.

Alice is clearly a competent communicator but the various creatures she encounters in *Wonderland* and *Through the Looking-Glass* challenge the basic premises upon which her competence is founded, above all the rules of polite conversation.

ALICE:—A knot? . . . oh do let me help to undo it.
THE MOUSE:—I shall do nothing of the sort. . . . You insult me by talking such nonsense.

[12] Judith Milner (1976).

THE HATTER:—Your hair wants cutting. . . .
ALICE:—You should learn not to make personal remarks. . . . It's very rude.

Another breach of convention is to give literal answers to questions:

ALICE:—I beg your pardon.
HUMPTY DUMPTY:—I'm not offended

or to answer by asking another question:

ALICE:—How am I to get in?
THE FOOTMAN:—Are you to get in at all?

which, as we all know, is simply not the done thing. In this way, the conflict between Alice and the strange world she is going through—whether it be Wonderland or Looking-Glass land—carries subtle information on how verbal interaction is carried out.

The linguistics of *langue*, indeed, cannot explain the diversity or complexity of the rules which govern address between speakers from different social groups or between members of the same group. Who does one address by name? Who does one address using a Christian name? Or title? Or prefix? What polite (or impolite!) formulas are to be used, with whom and in what circumstances? What power relationships are expressed through such usage—inferiority, equality, superiority; familiarity or distance—a usage which can be found codified, in various ways, in every society (be it caste society, class or classless society)? In order to achieve successful communication, speakers must assess the social role and status of each participant in the language event. In addition to status, sex and age are clearly important clues. Disagreement about status and role may result in conflict or a failure of communication. In addition to these speaker-related features, we need to consider the particular context of utterance. Obviously, we do not select the same register when we talk to our friends and family as when we deliver a lecture or a speech. Code-switching within a monolingual community is related to a scale of formality of speech events. In multilingual communities, the notion of code-switching extends to the choice of a particular language or variety of a language appropriate to the situation.

Every speaker, therefore, has a special kind of competence here, a *communicative* competence, which is rule-governed. The concept was introduced by Dell Hymes, the founder of the ethnography of speaking.

A normal child acquires knowledge of sentences, not only as grammatical, but also as appropriate. He or she acquires competence as to when to speak, when not, and as to what to talk about with whom, when, where, in what manner. In short, a child becomes able to accomplish a repertoire of speech acts, to take part in speech events, and to evaluate their accomplishment by others. This competence, moreover, is integral with attitudes, values, and motivations concerning language, its features and uses, and integral with competence for, and attitudes toward, the interrelation of language with the other codes of communicative conduct.[13]

Chomsky's *competence* or Saussure's *langue* are certainly useful abstractions: they allow us to define and clarify some universal, language specific phenomena. But they fail to give a complete picture of human language.[14] As Dell Hymes[15] puts it: 'There are rules of use without which the rules of grammar would be useless.'

[13] Dell Hymes (1972: 277-8).

[14] In recent years there has definitely been a shift from the view that syntax can and should be studied in isolation (the Chomskian position) to a pragmatic or sociolinguistic conception of linguistics incorporating the parameters of language use.

[15] 1972: 278.

11 Green Ideas
The Boundaries of Syntax and Semantics

> So far away
> From LA
> So far ago
> From Frisco
>
> All grammars leak
> (E. Sapir)

The grammar of a language is what enables us to create and understand well-formed sentences. For a sentence to be grammatical, it only needs to be recognized as such by the linguistic community on the basis of their intuition as native speakers. This intuition is based in the speakers' competence. There is no question, here, of introducing some social or cultural *norm* or of passing value judgements about 'fine language' or telling speakers how they *ought* to speak. The grammar that the linguist endeavours to describe is not a normative or prescriptive grammar, full of do's and don't's: 'different than' is just as grammatical as 'different from' and 'I can't see no one' as acceptable as ' I can't see anyone' or 'he talks real quick' as 'he talks really quickly'. The notion of a grammatical rule is supported by the usage common to a certain number of speakers, recognized as the only arbiters of grammaticality in their dialect. Whenever significant differences in usage are observed between different groups of speakers, no privilege should be given to the dominant group (the most educated or influential). The role of the linguist is to observe that there is such a thing as variation in any language, and this can, to a certain extent, be related to social, ethnic, or geographical differences. A language is no more than the sum of its various dialects. Dialects of the same language are defined as mutually intelligible varieties. If speakers of different dialects no longer understand one another, then the dialects in question must be considered as different languages, although this can be a tricky issue. Non-linguistic—political or cultural—criteria may interfere with linguistic ones, as in the current controversy over 'ebonics' (i.e. African-American Vernacular English) in the USA: is it a dialect of English or a language in its own right—thereby justifying the treatment of its speakers as a linguistic minority?

A dominant dialect, such as standard English or standard French, is often equated with *the* language on account of its status as the official medium of communication within a nation-state. It has been said that a language is 'a dialect with an army and a navy'[1] or 'a dialect which has succeeded'. Serbian and Croatian, clearly two dialects of the same language by linguistic criteria, are now to be considered as separate languages only because they are spoken by different armies.

The Three Levels of Grammar

Each one of us, while learning our native language, has internalized a language model, a three-tiered grammar, containing three levels: the level of meaning (semantics), the level of what is traditionally called 'grammar', i.e. morphology and syntax, and the level of sound patterns (phonology). I will adopt the viewpoint that anything which does not conform to any or all of these three components is ungrammatical or ill-formed, since the concept of grammar and hence of grammaticality encompasses all three levels.[2]

Consider this dialogue from Raymond Queneau's novel *Les Fleurs bleues*:

'Exkewsez noo,' said the male camper, 'mà wie sind perdus.'
'Nice start,' replied Cidrolin.
'Capito? Looorst . . . Perdustes.'
'What an *awful* fate.'
'Campigne? Lontano? Noo . . . smarriti . . . '
'He's a good talker', murmured Cidrolin, 'but is he speaking vernacular European or neo-Babelian?'
'Ah ha!' went the camper making gestures of clear and pronounced satisfaction. 'You fercht Iouropean?'
'Un poco', answered Cidrolin. 'Dump your kit here, noble foreign people and come have a boisson before you leave.'
'Ah ha! Capito: boisson . . . '
'Could they be Japanese?' pondered Cidrolin quietly. 'Yet they are blond of hair. Perhaps they're from Ainu?' So, addressing the boy, 'From Ainu by any chance?'
'Je? Non. Me: everybody's friend.'
'Oh I see: a pacifist.'
'Iawohl. What about the boisson?'
'Doesn't miss a trick, this European.'

This is a comic example of 'double Dutch'. We've all been confronted one day or another by foreigners struggling to make themselves understood and murdering the grammar of the language in various ways. The dialogue can be read as an absurd proof of the existence of linguistic competence. We

---

[1] This quote is often attributed to Max Weinreich, but it has also been attributed to Joshua Fishman and to Robert Hall.

[2] It is possible to restrict the notion of grammaticality to morphology and syntax.

understand very well—only a smattering of French, Italian, or German is required—and yet the text is clearly a morphological and syntactic monstrosity. The level of meaning is preserved, however, in spite of violations of form.

The phenomenon of *glossolalia* takes things one stage further: glossolalia is ecstatic speech in a non-existent language which some subjects produce in spite of themselves, in a kind of religious ecstasy. Examples can still be found in a number of religious sects where people 'speak in tongues'. While only temporary in religious delirium, glossolalia can be permanent in the most acute cases of aphasia.[3] Here is an example of the kind of language produced:

kolama siando, laboka tohoriamasi, lamo siando, laboka tahandoria, lamo siando kolamasi, labo siando, lakatandori, lamo siambaba katando, lama fia, lama fiandoriako, labokan doriasando, lamo siandoriako, labo sia, lamo siando[4]

In this case the de-structuration of language is total, it is bereft of all meaningful intentions and, consequently, of all semantic interpretation. It is completely ungrammatical.

Somewhere between Queneau's parodic intention, on the one hand, and involuntary glossolalia on the other, lies the methodical attempt recounted by Louis Wolfson in his *Le Schizo et les langues*. In his desire to destroy the English within him (which as his native language [mother tongue] he indentified with the hated mother figure), Wolfson began studying foreign languages, among them French (which he was later to adopt in order to talk about his experience), German, Russian, and Hebrew. He then perfected a system of elimination of English words using phonetic and semantic equivalents, building up a sort of personal Esperanto. A sentence like 'don't trip over the wire' became 'tu nicht [German] tre-bucher [French] über [German] èthhé [Hebrew] zwirn [German].'

The same phenomenon is sometimes found as a form of playful or cryptic language between individuals sharing the same bilingual or multilingual experience. For instance, the two young bilingual heroes of George du Maurier's *Peter Ibbetson*, communicate using a French and English pidgin called *Frankingle*—when the grammatical and phonetic base is English and the lexis French—or *Inglefrank*, when the reverse is true. For example, 'dispeach yourself to ferm the feneeter, Gogo. It geals to pierfend! We shall be inrhumed!' in Frankingle, becomes, in Inglefrank, 'Gogo, il frise à splitter les stonnes—maque aste et chute le vindeau; mais chute le donc vite! Je snize déjà!'

This last example highlights the relative autonomy—intuitively felt by most speakers—of grammatical structure and the lexicon: including the difference between structure words and content words, the latter only being

---

[3] See Sachs (1985: 8–9).   [4] Samarin (1972: 253).

affected by the children's special language. Syntax (word order, choice of structure words designed to indicate the function and class of the content words) and morphology (verb endings, markers for number and gender) ensure the apparent grammaticality of these utterances. Furthermore, borrowed words are made to conform to the phonological patterns of the borrower language, so that Frankingle sounds like English and Inglefrank like French. A related process was used by Anthony Burgess, in *A Clockwork Orange*, where words formed from slavic roots—and therefore completely incomprehensible for the vast majority of English readers—are incorporated into the English text. The *meaning* of these words is gradually clarified as the reader progresses, thanks to the comparisons s/he is can make between the different *functions* assumed by the same word in different contexts: which, in turn, allows the reader to identify the class of the word—noun, verb, adjective, etc. In this way, the reader, by a deductive process, gradually discovers the grammatical and semantic properties of the unknown words. Unwittingly, perhaps, s/he ponders a number of questions: do the words refer to animate beings or inanimate objects or entities? Do they refer to humans or non-humans? A word like *droog*, 'friend', will quickly be identified as 'human', since it is associated with verbs which require a human object or subject. One can also work out whether the words refer to male or female beings thanks to anaphoric pronouns (*he* versus *she*). Similarly, the structure of the sentence will indicate whether the words refer to the agents or instruments of an action; articles and markers for singular and plural will give the necessary clues as to whether the words are abstract or concrete, countable or uncountable:

Our pockets were full of deng, so there was no real need from the point of view of crasting any more pretty polly to tolchock some old veck in an alley and viddy him swim in his blood while we counted the takings and divided by four, nor to do the ultra-violent on some shivering starry grey-haired ptitsa in a sop and go secking off with the till's guts

Reading detective novels can sometimes pose the same type of problems for the reader, as can watching films about Chicago gangsters or Harlem thugs. Some frequently used terms have become familiar to us, *hoodlum*, *broad*, *dough*, *slug*, *plug*: others—*the Baker* (the electric chair), *cabbage* (paper money), *the Barrel* (prison)—we would find more difficult to understand: as indeed we might 'a heist in the keister' (a kick in the backside). Referring to a dictionary of slang is usually quite pointless, however, as the contextual parameters are enough to enlighten the non-slang-speaking reader. Our search for meaning is founded on grammatical competence.

For the *semantic* properties of words—and this is a very important point—are linked to their *syntactic* properties: that is, to the functions they can perform in the sentence. Syntactic slots—subject, object, indirect object—are filled by arguments whose definition is semantic—'agent', 'experiencer', 'patient', 'affected object', 'instrument', 'cause', 'goal', 'beneficiary', 'recipient', etc. It is clear that agency implies animacy while an affected object is normally inanimate. Such knowledge is crucial in determining that 'The child reads well' contains an agentive subject while 'The book reads well' does not or in accounting for the fact that 'Shakespeare reads very well' is an ambiguous sentence. A cause however can be either animate or inanimate. We could say 'Drinking from the bottle made Alice shrink' as well as 'The King made Alice laugh'.

The way we construct sentences thus depends on semantic roles. We may say for instance: 'The garden is swarming with bees' or alternatively 'Bees are swarming in the garden'. The noun-phrases *The garden* and *Bees* both fill the syntactic subject slot but must clearly be assigned a different semantic status.

Predicates are semantically characterized via *aspect*. We use aspect to convey that we are talking about a process or an act or a state or a property, about a general truth or a specific event; to express the way in which an action is performed, whether it is unique or repeated, short or prolonged, complete or incomplete, has a clear aim or is indeterminate and so on. In English for instance we can oppose:

The White Rabbit was running (indeterminate process)
The White Rabbit ran away (act)
The White Rabbit was a fine runner (property)
The White Rabbit kept running (continuous activity)
The White Rabbit has disappeared (resultant state)
The White Rabbit disappeared (event) etc.

All these distinctions belong in the semantic level of the grammar and must be congruent with the syntactic arrangement of sentences. Thus a syntactically well-formed sentence which, in the way it is put together, violates the selection restrictions based on the semantic properties of words, is just as ungrammatical as a sentence which, while having 'meaning', contains 'grammatical mistakes'. I return to this important point in more detail in a further section of this chapter. I also return to the relationship between syntax and semantics in the final chapter.

Grammaticality Judgements

There are important differences between the three tiers of the language model. Once the phonological system is in place, the speaker has very little latitude—except in such things as sound poems, electro-acoustic music and, of course, pathological cases of glossolalia. English speakers have internalized the rules that govern the combinations of phonemes that are licit in their language even though a number of these do not yield actual words. They do not produce, for example, illicit word-initial consonant clusters such as /nd/ or /nb/. Thus a street sign reading 'NDARY ROAD' will not fail to strike a native speaker of English as foreign.[5] (The said speaker can only feel relief when realizing that it is truncated from 'Boundary Road'.)

Syntax and semantics, on the other hand, are vulnerable to accidents of linguistic performance, to false starts as we have already seen. And they lend themselves to creativity and all kinds of transgressions.

Grammaticality is a fuzzy-edged concept. Theoretically, grammar (linguistic competence) generates only 'what we can say' and excludes 'what we can't say'. But the boundary between the two is not always clear-cut: the possible fades into the impossible, to the point where the acceptability of utterances in speakers' performance, as opposed to the grammaticality of sentences generated by competence, is often a matter of degree. When speakers are requested to pass grammaticality judgements based on their 'native speaker intuition' what they are really judging is utterances rather than abstract system sentences. Acceptability varies between speakers of the same language or dialect. It can be improved by context or intonation or communicative value. Acceptability judgements may also be influenced by social norms and prescription (the reference to rules taught at school, which have sometimes little to do with actual usage). Given that the native speaker is supposed to be always right about his or her language and given that attitudes to language vary enormously, eliciting consistent judgements can be a tricky task for the linguist, who is sometimes tempted to resort to his or her own intuition. A common statement in linguists' parlance is 'In *my* dialect, this is grammatical/ungrammatical' (as the case may be). Such statements are used as a hedge, to account for the uncomfortable fact that grammaticality judgements made by linguists do not always stand the test of judgements made by 'naive' native speakers.

How Ungrammatical Can You Get?

'Long time no see', says Lauren Bacall to Humphrey Bogart in a famous scene from *The Big Sleep*. This is a remark which is syntactically ill-formed but is endowed with meaning and quite deliberately produced. It has even become part of everyday usage. What we colloquially refer to as 'broken English' ensures a basic, if incorrect, communication. Newspaper headlines tend to remove redundant structure words in order to ensure maximum effi-

---

[5] This does not mean that the system is closed. Borrowed words introduce foreign phonological sequences: hence 'dj' in French—introduced via 'blue-jean' and 'jazz' or 'ing' introduced via 'parking' or again 'zz' via 'pizza'.

ciency in the message, thereby producing ill-formed sentences that are yet quite acceptable in their context: 'Inquiry into ticket fraud stalls rail sell-off'; 'French wine boycott successful'; 'Forbes shrugs off barbed attacks by White House rivals'. It is possible therefore to violate syntax and get away with it, i.e. achieve one's communicative aim. Poetry, on the other hand, in producing the unexpected, the impossible, the unheard of, seals redundancy's fate. By violating meaning, it reaches and sometimes breaches the limits of language.

What is there to stop us saying that 'colorless green ideas sleep furiously', the famous sentence coined by Chomsky as an example of semantic ungrammaticality? Dell Hymes proved the point in this poem:[6]

> Hued ideas mock the brain
> Notions of color not yet color
> Of pure and touchless, branching pallor
> Of an invading, essential green.
>
> Ideas, now of inchoate color
> Nest as if sleeping in the brain,
> Dormant, domesticated green,
> As if had not come a dreaming pallor
>
> Into the face, as if this green
> Had not, seeping, simmered, its pallor
> Seethed and washed throughout the brain,
> Emptying sense of any color.

Syntactic Anomalies

Antonin Artaud, André Breton, Robert Desnos, James Joyce, e. e. cummings, and Gertrude Stein, to name but a few, tried to break grammar up creatively, thereby questioning the function of communication based upon the norm or social consensus in which language is founded. The reason we recognize their work as art rather than gibberish is that some meaning is intended, even when it is based on organized deviance.

It is clear from the comparison of aphasic texts and poetic texts that these two forms of ungrammatical language are separated by *intention*.

Arthur Kopit's drama, *Wings*, is a conscious exploration of 'language disorder and its implications'. It is a work of imaginative speculation, but strongly informed by fact: the author's interest in the subject was prompted by the fact that his father suffered a stroke followed by aphasia. The character Kopit presents to us, Emily Stilson, has also had a stroke and appears

---

[6] In Sebeok (1960).

to suffer from *agrammaticism*, the form of aphasia which affects syntax, but leaves lexis untouched:

There I go there I go hallway now it's screaming crowded pokes me then the cool-breeze needle scent of sweetness can see palms flowers flummers couldn't fix the leaking sprouting everywhere to save me help me to something movement.[7]

Gertrude Stein, for her part, was a great practitioner of deliberately ungrammatical language.(She justified her approach at the theoretical level in her book *How to Write*.)

When he will see
When he will see
When he will see the land of liberty.
The scene changes it is a stone high up against with a hill and there is and above where they will have time. Not higher up below is a ruin which is a castle and there will be a color above it.[8]

And so was e. e. cummings:

> and like the prince of wales wife wants to die
> but the doctors won't let her comma considers frood
> whom he pronounces young mistaken and
> cradles in rubbery one somewhat hand
> the paper destinies of nations sic
> item a bounceless period unshy
> the empty house is full O Yes of guk
> rooms daughter item son a woopsing queer
> colon hobby photography never has plumbed
> the heights of prowst but respects artists if
> they are sincere proud of his scientif
> ic attitude and liked the king of)hear
>
> ye! the godless are the dull and the dull are the damned[9]

The following extract from *The Big Money* by John Dos Passos also strikes the reader as ungrammatical:

. . . the boy walks shyly browneyed beside me to the station talks about how Bart helped him with his homework wants to get ahead why should it hurt him to have known Bart? wants to go to Boston University we shake hands don't let them scare you accustomed the smokingcar accustomed the jumble of faces rumble cozily home-like towards Boston through the gathering dark how can I make them feel how our fathers our uncles haters of oppression came to this coast how say don't let them scare you . . .[10]

---

[7] From *Wings* (Kopit 1968: 25).   [8] From *How to Write* (Stein 1973: 13).
[9] 'proud of his scientific attitude', from *50 poems* (cummings 1939).
[10] John Dos Passos, *The Big Money*.

Syntactic anomalies, such as these can be assessed more easily than semantic ones, since our reaction consists, precisely, of a 'correction' of the devious utterance by reference to an internalized model of the grammar. The Dos Passos text for instance could certainly be made grammatical merely by inserting the proper punctuation and adding a couple of missing pronouns.

If correction proves impossible, then we simply reject the utterance as ungrammatical. This, for example, is our judgement when faced with the extract from *Wings*. But if we recognize poetic *intention*, as in the work of Stein or e. e. cummings, we have to *accept* syntactic anomaly as a legitimate form of expression. The difference between aphasic and poetic texts obviously lies in competence, not performance.

And yet, de-structuring language carries with it a number of risks. This is a journey into a space which falls outside social norms: and sometimes it is a one-way ticket. Certain psychedelic experiments bear witness to this, or the case of the French poet Antonin Artaud, who ultimately went mad, declaring 'all true language is incomprehensible'. The same might be said of Joyce: we no longer really know, from *Finnegans Wake* onwards, what the precise degree of intentionality is.

I shall return to the problem of syntax in more conventional uses of language in Chapter 14.

Semantic Anomalies

Semantic anomalies are infinitely more difficult to size up and do not lend themselves easily to correction: I mean by this, that the 'model' of semantic correction is not easy to define. Speakers tend to shrink from a semantic vacuum and are willing to try anything to conjure up meaning, even when it seems quite absurd. Moreover, breaking semantic rules is the legitimate preserve of imagery which, once lexicalized, leads to the evolution of a word's meaning (see below in Chapter 12).

In the light of various poetic examples it seems possible to distinguish three kinds of semantic anomalies: those deriving from the use of *forged lexicon*, those due to *breaches of logic*, and finally *violations of selection restrictions*. I shall take each of them in turn.

Linguistic Forgery

Here the utterance is meaningless or, in any event, there is no obvious meaning, since the words do not exist. This is mock poetry, such as Carroll's *Jabberwocky*.

> Twas brillig and the slithy toves
> Did gyre and gimble in the wabe

> All mimsy were the borogroves
> And the mome raths outgrabe

There is a long tradition of such forgery in literature. Henri Michaux's *The Great Fight*, in a translation which does justice to the original, is a good example:

> He embowerates and enbacks him on the ground.
> He raggs him and rumpets him up to his drale;
> He praggles him and libucks him and berifles his testeries;
> He tricards him and morones him,
> He grobels him rasp by rip and risp by rap.
> Finally, he enscorchorizes him.[11]

or Joyce in this excerpt from *Finnegans Wake*:

The wallhall's horrors of rollsrights, carhacks, stonegens, kisstvanes, tramtrees, fargobawlers, autokinotons, hippohobbilies, streefleets, tournintaxes, megaphoggs, circuses and wardsmoats and basilikerks and aeropagods.

Douglas Adams uses the same technique in *The Hitch-Hiker's Guide to the Galaxy*: 'And hooptiously drangle me with crinkly bindlewurdles or I will rend thee in the gobberwarts with my blurglecruncheon' (54). Again a parallel is found in certain language disorders: 'Well, all I know is somebody is clipping the kreples some where, someone here on the kureping arm, why I don't know'. This last utterance was produced by someone suffering from *jarganophasia*,[12] a form of aphasia which leaves grammatical structure intact, but dissolves lexis.

Breaches of Logic

An utterance may defy logic, especially the logic of presupposition, *implication*, and *incompatibility*.

Presupposition is that part of a message that does not need to be explicit because it is 'understood'. In the following quote from Carroll, the Footman is denying the validity of the presupposition underlying Alice's question, namely that she has the right to come in:

'How am I to get in?', asked Alice. . . .
'*Are* you to get in at all?' said the Footman. 'That's the first question, you know.' (46)

At the tea-party, when the March Hare says to Alice, 'Take some more tea' (58), he is assuming that she has already had some, whence Alice's confusion, her cup being quite empty. The logician in Carroll was fascinated by the absurd and by paradox.

---

[11] *Selected Writings of Henri Michaux* (Michaux 1952: 6–7).
[12] In Goodglass (1993: 86).

A common breach of logic is the so-called 'leading question', which sneaks in a covert presupposition as in: 'When did you stop beating your wife?'.

'Rodolph has killed his widow', transgresses the implication that a widow's husband is dead. 'Has your mother got any children?', violates the implication that a mother has children. A father saying of his daughter, 'I know her just as well as if I'd sired her', goes against similar fundamental implications. Or again, the headline in a French newspaper, 'Pope dies again', plays with the ambiguity of 'Pope' (referring to person or function) and violates the implication that you can only die once. Simone Signoret's autobiography, *Nostalgia Isn't What It Used To Be*, by modifying an aphorism, introduces an incompatibility. Indeed, this is a much favoured technique for forming titles which are catchy because they are unexpected: Kenneth Brannagh's film, *Dead Again*, or the James Bond adventure *You Only Live Twice*.

Tautologies also constitute violations of logic as in, 'you really are your father's son!', or the question put by the seasoned commuter: 'What time does the 5.15 for London leave?' Contradiction, as in 'The Living Dead', can take on a systematic character in *amphigoury* or tangle talk, a particular type of nonsense poetry, very popular with schoolchildren:

> I went to the pictures tomorrow
> I took a front seat at the back
> I fell from the pit to the gallery
> And broke a front bone in my back
> A lady she gave me some chocolate
> I ate it and gave it her back
> I phoned for a taxi and walked it
> And that's why I never came back[13]

In all of these authentic examples—lines of verse, titles of films, TV programmes, books, headlines, proverbs, everyday expressions—the ungrammatical language is deliberate and designed to make sense out of nonsense.

Violation of Semantic Selection Restrictions

This has been explored, in different ways, by the Surrealists and by OULIPO: the former placing themselves in the hands of creative chance, the latter systematically applying a method. The French Surrealists enjoyed playing a game called 'cadavre exquis' ('exquisite corpse'), which assembles totally unrelated elements into sentences by passing round a piece of paper which is carefully folded over each time to hide the preceeding contribution; this results in breaches of semantic compatibility (i.e. violations of semantic selection restrictions), since the players do not have available a set of

---

[13] Peter and Iona Opie (1959: 24–5).

combinatorial constraints which could ensure the grammaticality of the utterance they are producing (one cannot put any determinant before any noun, any noun before any verb, and so on). William Burroughs achieved very similar results with his cut-ups.

Surrealist poetry, of course, has from its beginnings sought to liberate the human unconscious in acts of 'automatic' writing: it produces incongruous associations and evokes unpremeditated images, as in Breton's 'drawers of flesh with handsfull of hair', 'a subterranean passage unites all perfumes' or 'the circus always enchants the same tramlines'.[14] Gavin Ewart—to quote a Surrealist poet writing in English—provides a good example of the outcome in *Lines*:

> The other day I was loving a sweet little fruitpie-and-cream
> He was flying an Avro-Manhattan into a beady-eyed silence.
> His little shoes were shining as he stood by the sealions.
> Panting she lifted her skirt in a classical gesture.[15]

What is in question in all of these more or less bizarre productions are the rules of selection which ordinarily eliminate incompatible combinations of words, on the basis of their semantic properties or features, even if the syntactic organization of the utterance seems 'correct'.

This last kind of semantic violation, especially, invites us to call into question the separateness, or autonomy of 'syntax': for syntax must clearly also take in the rules governing semantic selection. It is not enough to sort words into classes: verbs, nouns, adverbs, and so on, or to specify the different constructions which are possible. We need also to be able to formulate rules which would allow us to eliminate utterances like those I have just been quoting, or at least allow us to assess these as creative deviance. That is we need rules which specify the overall properties or semantic features of each word, features which allow it, say, to occupy the position of agentive subject of a transitive verb, but not that of affected object. Put simply, how do we account for the fact that we can say 'John admires sincerity', but not 'Sincerity admires John'? And here, whether we like it or not, we reintroduce the notion of norm and deviance.

Semantic Features

From a technical point of view, semantic analysis borrows the techniques of phonological analysis. Just as a phoneme is composed of a cluster of distinctive features which can be analysed, but not divided, since they form one and the same phonic reality, so a word, too, is composed of a cluster of *semes*, or semantic features whose combination results in rules of selection:

[14] *Surrealist Poetry in English* (Germain 1978: 116–17).   [15] Ibid. 285.

rules which constitute the semantic structure of the language. Breaking these rules produces ungrammatical sentences. The phonological system allows certain combinations (the knowledge of which constitutes phonological competence) while excluding others. One would like to believe that the same is true of the semantic system. Features are ascribed to words in the lexicon, usually in binary fashion: animate/inanimate, human/non-human, material/non-material, male/female, adult/non-adult, mortal/non-mortal, unique/non-unique, etc. The 'etc.' proves quite useful, for the list would otherwise be difficult to bring to a close. Two important principles help to delimit the list: features should be as general as possible, and they should be genuinely semantic. Thus we can point out the following dangers:

1. The danger of introducing ad hoc features, valid for special cases but not generalizable at all. What use is an ungeneralizable rule? For example, we would not want to account for the anomalous status of 'Mary's widower is here', by ascribing to *widower* a specific feature 'incompatible with a possessive noun phrase'.[16]

2. The danger of mistaking parameters which are peculiar to our culture and our vision of the world for semantic features: that is, the danger of confusing the extra-linguistic world—the referent—with the linguistic system, whose autonomy we have been at such pains to demonstrate. For speakers, semantic 'normality' is often nothing more than the reflection of a vision of the world which demands that an utterance have *reference*, if it is to have a *meaning*: a vision which seems to reject devious usage. In this scheme of things, any utterance would be semantically ill-formed if the average speaker were unable to interpret it, because s/he was unable to find a referent in the real world as it presents itself to consciousness.

Referential vs. Semantic Anomalies

It is quite difficult to distinguish between *semantic* anomalies, those which result from breaches of the semantic structure of the language and *referential* anomalies. And yet this distinction is crucial. The fact that we find such and such a situation inconceivable is not in itself enough to deem ungrammatical an utterance which gives an account of it. Galileo's sentence 'the Earth revolves' was clearly, at the time, a referential anomaly. By the same token, 'the Earth is flat and lies motionless in space', is anomalous for us today. Referential anomalies ascribe properties to objects and to beings

---

[16] Cf. R. Lakoff (1975). The phrase 'Mary's widower' is unacceptable for social reasons associated with the pre-eminent status of men in our society, a status which does not admit the definition of men in relation to women. 'Mary's widower', therefore, can only be interpreted as an attack on the social order which justifies its being excluded from usage.

which remain unverified in the normal world as we perceive it. But I have already stressed that reference must be distinguished from meaning. John Lyons[17] states the case with his usual sense of humour:

'The horse miaowed' is surely to be regarded as semantically well formed, on the grounds that it expresses a proposition that we could, not only rationally discuss, but even verify. We should be surprised, of course, if we actually found in the world in which we live our everyday lives a horse that miaowed rather than neighed. But that is beside the point. We could identify a horse miaowing, if we ever came across one.

We all have the right to create a world in which the laws of the universe are suspended. In Alice's world, animals talk. This is a referential anomaly which leads to the construction of a fictional world in which it becomes normal to encounter the sentence: 'the White Rabbit said . . . ', whereas *say* typically takes a human subject. But this does not change the meaning of the verbs *say* or *speak* or *tell* at all and they are not reinterpreted. On the contrary, the selection restriction rules are breached if, in order to be interpreted, the utterance requires us not to believe in an imaginary world, but to *recategorize* the offending word. Such semantic violations are at the heart of what we call metaphor. *I could murder a curry* does not mean that *curry* has been promoted to the status of 'human': the verb *to murder* is simply reinterpreted as a metaphor meaning 'to eat voraciously/with great enthusiasm'. The same might be said of expressions such as *eat up the miles, swallow one's pride, chew on a problem,* and so on: it would not occur to anyone to interpret these idioms literally. And no native speaker would reject them as ungrammatical.

Language has the power to create its own categories. If we exclude 'eating man is good for you', it is solely for cultural reasons. What we reject as anomalous is the content, i.e. the reference, of this statement. We find it unpalatable (no joke intended). However, linguistically, the fact of using the word *man* in this context simply makes it into an uncountable noun, a material mass, putting it in the same class as *chicken* or *sugar*. And it makes perfect sense.

During the course of the banquet after the game of chess which makes Alice Queen, she is introduced, most ceremoniously, to a leg of mutton in front of her on the table:

'You look a little shy: let me introduce you to that leg of mutton,' said the Red Queen. 'Alice—Mutton: Mutton—Alice.'

And because of the introduction, the leg of mutton assumes the characteristic 'animate' (almost human, in fact). Thus, when Alice, addressing the Queen, offers her a slice, the Queen replies indignantly:

'Certainly not . . . it isn't etiquette to cut anyone you've been introduced to.' (200)

[17] 1977: ii. 420.

with *anyone* referring back to the leg of mutton. What Lewis Carroll is illustrating, in comic fashion, is language's ability to categorize: paradoxically, as it happens, since the English lexicon separates terms which refer to living animals and terms referring to the meat obtained from them.[18]

The Rules of Semantic Transfer

Utterances like 'he's a big girl's blouse' or 'he's a sissy' or 'he's a wet blanket' are not semantically abnormal. The boundary between 'animate' and 'inanimate' or between 'male' and 'female' may seem to be crossed. But we operate a mechanism of *semantic transfer* which, while preserving intact the semantic composition of 'girl's blouse' or 'blanket', alerts us to the fact that they are being used metaphorically, in a figurative sense and that it is precisely the properties of the terms used which are most incompatible with *he* which reveal the semantic intention. Pejorative terms, insults, very often consist of such semantic transfers. For example, English operates a certain number of distinctions in its lexical system on the basis of the opposition between human and non-human:

human	*non-human*
nose	snout
legs	shanks
hands	paws
feet	paws
hips	flanks
bottom	rump
kill	slaughter
kill	put down
corpse	carion
give	birth litter

Hence the pejorative value of the non-human term being applied in a human context: 'spindle shanks'; 'get your snout out of my dinner'; 'get your mucky paws off me'; 's/he ought to be put down'; 'they were not killed, they were slaughtered'. In fact, the language of contempt, of insults, is systematically derived from such semantic transfer—a decidedly useful mechanism. One sometimes wonders, indeed, if there is any limit to images designed to insult. Almost any term, it would seem, can be used as an insult,

---

[18] Historically, of course, this distinction stems from the borrowing of French words to designate the meat eaten by Norman barons, while the Saxon peasantry continued to call their animals by their native names, whence the lexical pairs: *calf—veal*; *sheep—mutton*; *ox—beef*; *pig—pork*.

provided it is placed within an appropriate syntactic frame: 'you steaming great . . . sugar bowl, you!'; 'you stupid cold frame'.

Semantic anomalies make demands on a speaker's interpretive abilities, opening up the possibility of imagery. It is impossible to account for the conceptual and logical structure of meaning without also taking into account figures of speech (metaphor, metonymy, hyperbole, irony, etc.). If one is so disposed, anything can be interpreted. Thanks to the mechanism of transfer, the semantic structure of the language seems to be in a constant state of flux. Ultimately, semantic anomaly does not exist. If, for instance, I hear someone say 'John has finally been cured of his incurable sickness'—seemingly a contradiction in terms—I could interpret this as an ironical statement: perhaps John is a hypochondriac, at length delivered from his false notions by means of a well-conducted psychoanalysis. Or perhaps John is just workshy. 'Rodolph has killed his widow', could mean that the memory or ghost of her husband has brought about the death of the unfortunate woman. It is a well-known fact that the prisoners in Soviet labour camps were wont to refer to their wives as 'my widow'. 'To suffer a thousand deaths', is not taken to be contradictory, but as an instance of hyperbole, implying a displacement of the meaning of *death*.

When Chomsky produced his famous 'colorless green ideas sleep furiously' as an example of a semantically ill-formed sentence this was taken as a challenge by a number of linguists and several tried to prove him wrong in more or less jocular fashion. Besides Dell Hymes's poem quoted above, the most successful attempt is this little fable by Y. R. Chao:[19]

'Making Sense out of Nonsense: the Story of my Friend, Whose Colorless Green Ideas Sleep Furiously':

> I have a friend who is always full of ideas, good ideas and bad ideas, fine ideas and crude ideas, old ideas and new ideas. Before putting his new ideas into practice, he usually sleeps over them, to let them mature and ripen. However, when he is in a hurry, he sometimes puts his ideas into practice before they are quite ripe, in other words, while they are still green. Some of his green ideas are quite lively and colorful, but not always, some being quite plain and colorless. When he remembers that some of his colorless ideas are still too green to use, he will sleep over them, or let them sleep, as he puts it. But some of those ideas may be mutually conflicting and contradictory, and when they sleep together in the same night they get into furious fights and turn the sleep into a nightmare. Thus my friend often complains that 'his colorless green ideas sleep furiously'.

This is a very elaborate and far-fetched example of how *acceptability* can be contrived by constructing an adequate context. But it does show that while it is possible to separate *syntactic* ill-formedness from *semantic* ill-

---

[19] As collected on the World Wide Web at: http://weber.U.Washington.edu./~yuenren/green ideas. html.

formedness (which was the point Chomsky was making when he produced his monster of a sentence) the latter is more difficult to establish than the former.

Any utterance can be justified by the meaning it produces. Meaning, in its most general sense, is essentially contextual, linked to the intentions of the speaker and the conditions of communication: in short, to *speech*. The search for the semantic 'norm' at the abstract level of the language system can be justified in theoretical terms—despite the problems it raises—because it helps us to distinguish clearly the different phenomena under discussion. However, what interests us, above all, are the mechanisms which allow us to transgress the norm—mechanisms whose very existence is axiomatic—and yet still produce meaning, that is interpretable and acceptable utterances.

How does the creativity of speech work, as opposed to the 'normality' of the language system? Like Saussure, we could push everything deviant into the domain of speech, 'parole', or individual performance. And yet, the organizing principles which produce this apparent disorder are systematic and rule-governed and must therefore be accounted for within competence. The language system, we have to conclude, must also contain rules which allow and govern the transgression of its own structure. Moreover, these transgressions throw light on the nature of language, how it works, how meaning is created and on the relation of the speaker to language: 'what you *can't* say', that is, is a privileged method for finding out the rules which organize 'what you *can* say'.

12   Murdering Time
Figures of Speech

'Off with his head! He is murdering Time'

'It was a book to kill time for those who like it better dead.'

'Such is the strange condition of language', wrote the French poet Jean Paulhan in *Le Don des langues* ('The Gift of Languages'), 'that there isn't a single word which doesn't carry within itself the seeds of its own destruction and, as it were, a kind of mechanism for overturning its initial meaning': the language which outlaws figures of speech does not exist.

Figurative meaning is produced, as we have just seen, whenever semantic rules are broken, whenever the boundaries between animate and inanimate, human/non-human, material/non-material and so on are crossed or ignored. Idioms such as, *babbling brook, killing time, whispering grass, walls have ears* and so on, all use *transferred* semantic features. And this does not have to imply any poetic effect or intention. The whole of language is overrun by figures of speech, regardless of whether the motivation is aesthetic or utilitarian. The effects may be different, but the mechanism is the same.

The figurative use of language, then, results in shifts of meaning. Metaphor, metonymy, and synecdoche—the three most common figures—all rest on the two main organizing principles of language: selection (on the paradigmatic or vertical axis) and combination (along the syntagmatic or horizontal axis). Metaphor relies on a relationship of resemblance—whether imaginary or real—while metonymy and synecdoche rely on a relationship of contiguity.

Expressions such as *killing time, money-laundering, Pound struggles against Mark, prices collapse, profits soar, share prices quiet* are all *metaphors*, a figurative term having been substituted for a literal one in the vertical axis. On the other hand, *ski sale* ('skiing equipment'), *Do you like Brahms?* ('Brahms's musical works'), *I'm reading Shakespeare* ('the works of William Shakespeare') *the back row was noisy* ('people sitting in the back row'), *there were lively reactions from the floor* ('from people sitting in the audience') are all examples of *metonymy*. Expressions such as *a pint, a mink, the Crown, the East Stand, the House of Commons, the strings,* and so on, are examples of *synecdoche*. Metonymy, like synecdoche, uses an ellipsis on the syntagmatic axis, a single word representing a group of words. The two figures are often lumped together under the heading *metonymy*, but can be distinguished though not always clearly—by the fact that in metonymy, the relationship between the two words where one includes the other, is *external*. With synecdoche, on the other hand, the relationship is an *internal* one: we take the part for the whole, the container for the contents (or the other way around), the substance for the object made of it, the characteristic for the object which exhibits it.

Metaphor appears to have the greatest poetic potential, in the sense that it necessarily leads to the symbolic use of language and to frequently unexpected juxtapositions. Metonymy and synecdoche, on the other hand, being elliptical, seem to follow the line of least resistance and are often a form of abbreviation, or a way of taking advantage of redundancy. When not frozen into an idiom, metaphor, as with all poetic language, is a challenge to redundancy. Its power of expression is therefore all the greater.

   Q: *What has an eye but cannot see?*
   A: *A needle.*

The *eye of a needle* and *the eye of the storm*, do not have the same value as figures of speech. The former is compulsory, while the latter is free. In the case of free figures, one signifier is substituted for another and an expressive or symbolic parallel is drawn: but the signified remains the same. In the case of compulsory figures, a signifier has its signified extended or displaced, in order to respond to revised communication needs. The *wing* of a car or a plane, the *wing* of a large house, or of an army in battle, or on a football pitch, all derive from the original meaning of 'a bird's wing': but they are all compulsory figures of speech, since there are no alternative words available for the derived uses. The *leg* of a table, the *arm* of a chair, the *jacket* of a book, the *back* of a box, the *cap* of a pen, the *hand* of a clock, and so on, were originally metaphors, since they are based on a likeness. But they are now devoid of all expressive value, since that would imply that a choice was available. An expressive value is only obtained when we realize that the meaning of an utterance is deviant and that a poetic effect or a joke is intended: only then do we search for an interpretation via the semantic transfer rule.

We should perhaps now explore how the semantic transfer rule actually operates in practice. It seems to be the case that each anomaly of meaning is decoded in two separate stages:

   (1) The anomaly is perceived. We note the incompatibility on the syntagmatic axis—in terms, that is, of contiguity relations—and the fact, therefore, that the rules of selection have been broken.
   (2) We then explore the paradigmatic axis, searching among the relations of likeness, in order to find an acceptable substitute.

For example: 's/he has green ideas'. *Green* is perceived as incompatible with *ideas* which, because it contains the semantic feature 'non-material', excludes adjectives of colour. Therefore (moving on to the second stage), we begin looking for an acceptable substitute for *green*. The value of *green* as symbolic of nature, combined with the current ideological climate, enable us to interpret the word as an *ecological* signifier. At the outset, *green ideas* is an invented image, with expressive value. This new meaning of *green*, however, is very quickly generalized and adopted in everyday usage: *Green Party, green policies, green consumers, green products, the green pound*, and so on. *Green* takes on the meanings of 'marginal', 'ecological', 'natural', or 'having some connection with agriculture'. With time, *green ideas* becomes lexicalized to the same extent as *black eye, blue blood, blue film, blue note, in the red, red cent, yellow bellied*, and so on. The new meaning then must be considered as part of the signified and included in the dictionary—an instance of creative language use having a retroactive effect on the language system.

An anomaly ceases to be felt as such when it moves into general use. The semantic structure of the language system is then modified. When this happens, an image is said to be 'dead' (an expression which, in itself, constitutes a dead metaphor), the 'burial' place being the dictionary: note the use of inverted commas or 'scare quotes' here (a trick much abused by journalists) to denote that this last image is not yet dead.

We only have to listen to people talking, or study the history of language a little, to realize that a surprisingly large number of idiomatic phrases, in fact, derive from figures of speech: *to accost a passer-by, broad in the beam, to get into deep water, hit the deck, to take the wind out of someone's sails, to throw someone a line, two ships that pass in the night*, and now *surfing the Net*: English is full, not to say overflowing with these and many more marine or seafaring metaphors. But how many of us still really perceive them as such? A metaphor can even have its meaning turned on its head: it is not infrequent to hear of an athlete or a racing driver leaving another 'in his wake', the maritime origins of the expression being transferred to dry land. Conversely, ships described as 'ploughing through heavy seas' transfer an agricultural term into the maritime . . . field (yet another dead metaphor!).

Unnoticed by most of us, military metaphors have taken over political and trade-union rhetoric: one is tempted to say that they have occupied or conquered it. The Prime Minister or Leader of the Opposition is often described as *mustering his troops for the forthcoming battle*, by issuing a *rallying cry* and then *fixing his sights on the enemy*. The same can also be said of sport. A cricket captain may have as his *main weapon* a fast bowler who *bombards* an unfortunate batsman, only to see the latter *fire a superb shot*, which goes like a *rocket* for four. On the other hand, war and military action can be referred to in terms of games or gambling, involving *moving pawns, bluffing, playing by the rules, cheating, taking risks*, and so on:

In gambling, to achieve certain 'gains', there are 'stakes' that one can lose. When one asks what is 'at stake' in going to war, one is using the metaphors of Causal Commerce and Risks-as-Gambles. These are also the metaphors that President Bush uses when he refers to strategic moves in the Gulf as a 'poker game' where it would be foolish for him to 'show his cards', that is to make strategic knowledge public.[1]

Metaphor can also be grounded in connotation. Certain words acquire a symbolic value for speakers of particular societies. The names of animals, for example, very often have a symbolic connotational value: hence the frequent metaphors motivated by the anthropomorphic qualities we attribute to animals (a relationship exploited by the writers of fables). So it is that we can refer to someone as a *shark* or a *snake*, for example. The sentence 'that man is a pig' is therefore possible because the connotations of the lexical *notion* of *pig* include negative physico-cultural properties such as dirtiness and vulgarity. Such values can vary from one language to another: while the police are *poulets* ('chickens') in French, they are *pigs* in English. Not all animal names lend themselves to metaphor, since the symbolic interpretation depends on a cultural consensus. *You are an absolute rat*, for example, is quite acceptable, but *you are an absolute stegosaurus* is far less so: we should be hard pressed to define the physico-cultural properties of a stegosaurus.[2] Nonetheless we would probably perceive this as an insult, since most sentences with the form *X is an absolute Y* are insults.

Metaphors in foreign languages strike us more than they do in our native language because they are unfamiliar to us. In Amerindian languages the train is called the 'iron horse': in neo-Melanesian pidgin, hair is *grass bilong head* and a beard is *grass bilong face*. 'How exotic', we think, not realizing, perhaps, that these are compulsory figures of speech and are therefore not perceived by speakers as metaphors any more than *flower beds* are by English speakers. Once lexicalized, such figures of speech are no longer noticed—whether they were free or compulsory at the outset. But this does not contradict the assertion that metaphor and metonymy constitute the main mechanisms by which meaning is extended. They therefore play a crucial role in the development of language.

The lexicalization of a figure of speech can be considered complete when the replacement of the figurative term by a synonym or near synonym surprises us or makes us laugh. This is a frequent source of humour (sometimes deliberate, but often unintentional where children or foreigners are concerned), as in: *apple roll-over* for *apple turnover*; *vocal strings* for *vocal cords*; *crazy ox disease* instead of *mad cow disease*, or *murdering time* for *killing time*. Or again, there may be a slight modification in the syntax of a saying,

---

[1] In George Lakoff, *Metaphor in Politics* (1991), an open letter to the Internet.
[2] See Leech (1974: 214).

like *fine words do not butter the parsnips*, instead of *fine words butter no parsnips*.

In *Through the Looking Glass* and *Alice's Adventures in Wonderland*, Carroll very often takes metaphors literally, a technique which helps to create a world whose logic is different from our own, thereby underlining violations of the semantic structure of words, which is precisely what makes our figures of speech possible. For example, the phrase *killing time*, no longer perceived as an image by speakers, is taken literally. But *kill* implies an animate object. Time, with a capital T, thus becomes a living character, a character whose existence is made necessary by the semantic constraints of the verb *kill*, which can then be replaced by *murder*: 'Off with his head', cries the Queen, 'he's murdering Time'. As for the talking flowers, their status as living beings derives from the words *flower bed*. Beds are for sleeping in and to sleep you must be alive, and this is what makes the flowers speak: in the real world, beds are soft, so flowers are always asleep. But in Wonderland, flower beds are hard and keep the flowers awake.

Semantic transfers of the kind we are discussing often happen in a series, with each of the successive, essentially metonymical shifts of meaning forming a link in the chain. If we take the word *seat*, for example, we have: 'a piece of furniture on which one sits'; but also 'the part of the body which does the sitting', as in the quip, 'would you please take your seats and place them on the chairs behind you'; and finally, 'what covers that part of one's body' (the seat of a pair of trousers); in addition, any fixed place, especially for a number of important public functions—throne, court, see, constituency.

The word *film*, to take another example, illustrates the metonymic chain as extended by modern technology. Initially derived from an old Frisian word meaning 'skin', the word acquired the meaning 'membrane', was then extended to cover the notion of 'mist' or 'haze', then a thin silk-like or gossamer screen or 'coating'. From there, it was a relatively small step to designate, using the same term, the thin layer of light-sensitive emulsion on a photographic plate. Further metonymic extensions soon added cinematographic uses of the word: an event recorded on celluloid; the celluloid roll itself; the entire cinematographic industry. As we can see, there is a considerable difference between the initial meaning of the word and the last one listed here. Indeed, in some cases, the chain of meanings can be rather difficult to account for, since the metonymical or metaphorical link unifying the different meanings is often far from obvious in a *synchronic* context, that is the context of the contemporary language, which alone has any reality for the average speaker. However, well-worn metaphor, because of its symbolic value, proves more easily identifiable than metonymy. In metonymic chain-shifts, the relationship between the latest sense and the original one is usually lost.

An interesting consequence of this mechanism by which chains of meaning are formed, is that it is very rare to find words in two different languages whose meanings exactly coincide. Every language plays independently with its figures of speech and continually readjusts the way it conceptualizes the world (see Chapter 7). Even in the case of two languages with closely related histories and many words of common origin, or even when two languages borrow from each other extensively—as English and French do—we note important differences in the spectrum of meaning: it is usually one restricted meaning of a word which is borrowed. Once integrated into the borrowing language, the words begin a career of their own. Thus in trendy, popular French, the verb louser /luze/, from the English verb *to lose*, has the restricted sense of 'to be a loser' and can only be used intransitively as in *j'ai lousé* ('I lost out'). Similarly, *rapper* has only the limited meaning 'to practise the art of rap': a *bit* is only used in French in computing; *crawl* designates only a swimming stroke, *surf* a type of sport.

Modern English creates new technical terms essentially through metaphor, while French tends to use neologisms from Greek or Latin roots: compare, for example, English *painkiller* and French *analgésique*. But French increasingly borrows technical terms from English instead of coining neologisms. However, a French speaker using the journalese *scoop*, from *to scoop* ('to empty out', 'to dig out'), is entirely unaware that it is a metaphor, just as in the case of such computing terms as *hardware* or *software* or *to surf the Net* ('surfer sur le net').

The range of effects which images produce, in different languages, is sometimes a source of amusing mistakes. In French a table has *feet* not *legs* and a clock has *needles* not *hands*, while in both languages a chair may have *arms*.

When we talk about figures of speech, we should resist the temptation to think of 'style', or 'rhetoric', 'literary language', 'fine language'. Figurative language exists in every register, every style, even the most pragmatic and prosaic. Indeed one of the main ways in which slang is formed is through figurative speech: criminals, for example, refer to prison warders as *screws*; time spent in prison is *porridge* or *bird* (lime); weapons are *tools*; the police are *pigs* or *the filth*; a colleague who disposes of your stolen goods for you is a *fence*. Both formal and popular language make use of figures of speech. The language of the market-stall owner or the sports writer is peppered with images, not just that of the Oxbridge graduate, the politician, or the Professor.

To summarize, we can identify three different types of figurative language, according to their role in a language at any one point in time:

(1) compulsory and free figures which have become lexicalized: these are largely responsible for polysemy, to which I return in the next chapter;

(2) free figures still perceived as such, but having the status of idioms. These are often a source of unintentional humour and give rise to 'howlers';

(3) creative figures, seen conventionally as the privilege of poets, are often also found in the speech of children, in whom semantic categories are not yet properly established—especially the distinction between animate/inanimate. Children often produce them quite spontaneously, as in 'taking the hat/coat off a lolly' (by contrast, *a coat of paint* is a fixed image).

13

The Miser and the Prodigal Son
Lexical Meaning

Mirrors would do well to reflect before showing us our image

(Jean Cocteau)

The Miser: Polysemy and Homonymy

The process of semantic transfer may result in polysemy and ambiguity. Through this process (discussed in Chapter 11), the creative language-user generates mystery and surprise and it is often the hearer's job to come up with a personal interpretation or one derived from the context. But, as we saw in the previous chapter, the lexicalization process legitimizes polysemy, and gives multiple meanings a permanent place within the language.

From a purely utilitarian point of view, polysemy—(as well as homophony which we shall look at in a moment)—amounts to an economy in the number of signs used, evoking the image of the miser. Several different signifieds can correspond to the same signifier. The price we have to pay for this is the risk of ambiguity, a feature systematically exploited by cross-word compilers and the mainspring of the riddles handed down from generation to generation of schoolchildren:

Q: What's the difference between an engine-driver and a schoolmaster?
A: One minds the train, the other trains the mind,

Q: Why is it hard for a leopard to hide in the jungle?
A: 'Cause he's always spotted.

Q: When is an artist unhappy?
A: When he draws a long face.

Q: What makes the Tower of Pisa lean?
A: It doesn't eat enough.

Q: Why is a nobleman like a book?
A: Because he has a title.

Q: What's worse than raining cats and dogs?
A: Hailing taxis.

The French humorist Tristan Bernard is famous for his definition of *entracte* ('intermission'): 'vide [empties] les baignoires et remplit [fills] les lavabos', where *baignoire* 'bath tub' also means 'a ground-floor box in a theatre' (via metaphor) and *lavabo* 'wash-basin' can be a euphemism for a public loo (via metonymy).

A manipulation of polysemy often exploited in maxims or aphorisms is the rhetorical device called *antanaclasis*: 'In thy youth learn some craft, that in thy old age thou mayest get thy living without craft', or 'the heart of the matter is often a matter of the heart'. We see a more extended example in this article from a leading French newspaper:

The President, playing on words, told us that he had not spoken of Palestinian self-determination out of interest, but only in France's interest. In fact, if we take some interest, or even have some interest in this problem, it is because this concerns our country's higher interest which, for once, equates with the general interest. But it is also the case that our interest in OPEC, above and beyond simply showing an interest, encourages us to believe that we will make some interest out of oil. So much so, that the President—and it would not have been entirely without interest—might have admitted to us that, in seeking to arouse the interest of the UAE, he was also seeking to write a page of history, full of interest.[1]

Zeugma is a figure of speech which consists of associating a verb with two or more words which, although individually compatible with the verb used, are incompatible when they occur together: 'to open the window and one's heart', 'he swallowed his pride and a cough lozenge', 'Mr Pickwick took his hat and his leave', or Pope's

> Whether the Nymph shall break Diana's Law,
> Or some frail China jar receive a Flaw,
> Or stain her Honour, or her new Brocade,
> Forget her Pray'rs, or miss a Masquerade,
> Or lose her Heart, or Necklace, at a Ball[2]

In each of these examples the comic effect stems from the contrast between a *figurative* use of the verb within a set phrase or idiom (*to open one's heart, to swallow one's pride, to take one's leave, to lose one's heart*) and a *literal* use of the same verb.

Polysemy is a source of ambiguities, whether deliberate or not. Homophony and paronymy, on the other hand, lend themselves better to punning. Though both polysemy and homonymy, when they involve the same spelling for two different words or different senses of one word, are essential for such things as crosswords, the purely oral humour of puns—and the reason why psychoanalysts take such delight in them (see Chapter 6)—lies in

---

[1] From *Le Monde*, Mar. 1990.   [2] *The Rape of the Lock*, ii, 105–9.

the unexpected or chance juxtaposition of sounds and meanings. Often, however, the more tenuous the pun, the better it is, since attention is drawn to the deliberate distortion which has taken place. One could argue that Lewis Carroll's best puns are also his worst:

Then a very gentle voice in the distance said, 'She must be labeled "Lass, with care", you know.' (131).

'Well, there was Mystery,' the Mock Turtle replied, counting off the subjects on his flappers, 'Mystery, ancient and modern, with Seaography: then Drawling—the Drawling master was an old conger eel, that used to come once a week: he taught us Drawling, Stretching and Fainting in Coils'. (76-7)

'That's the reason they're called lessons,' the Gryphon remarked, 'because they lessen from day to day.' (77)

Homophones (i.e. homonyms with a different spelling), as exploited in children's word games provide a way of learning through play, the aim being to attract the attention of young schoolchildren to problems of meaning, but also of spelling:

Q: What's the difference between a cat and a comma?
A: A cat has its *claws* at the end of its *paws* and a comma has its *pause* at the end of its *clause*.

or, to take a well-known French example:

Il était une *fois*, dans la ville de *Foix*, une marchande de *foie*, qui vendait du *foie*, elle se dit: 'ma *foi*, c'est la dernière *fois* . . .

Homophony between common and proper nouns can also produce some confusing situations, as Messrs Watt and Knott discover to their cost during an unfortunate telephone call:

'Hello. Who's speaking please?'
'Watt,' a man answered.
'What's your name?' said Mr Knott.
'Yes. Watt's my name,' was the answer. 'Are you Jack Smith?'
'No, I'm Knott.'
'Will you give me your name, please?' said Mr Watt.
'Will Knott.'

The line between polysemy and homonymy/homophony is not always very clear. Children of pre-school age, or someone who is illiterate cannot possibly have the same perception of these linguistic features as an adult who has mastered the spelling system. In fact, where puns and wordplay are concerned, no distinction is made between the three features. To make the difference clear we would need to refer to the history of the language, as revealed through spelling, as we saw in Chapter 6. Leaving that aspect to one side, however, the problem can be expressed as a very simple opposition between:

(1) those cases where speakers are aware that they are using the 'same' word with different meanings (polysemy);

(2) cases where speakers are aware of using different, quite distinct words, whether spelled the same or not, and between which they would not establish any etymological or logical link (*wear, ware, where, we're,* for example).

An original case of polysemy will become a case of homonymy when speakers no longer have any sense of the metaphorical or metonymical link between the original meaning and the derived meanings: that is, when images are not simply dead, but buried so deep that we can no longer work out where they came from. Quite often, when we consider a word from the point of view of the present-day language, there appear to be two words (homonyms), which are really a single, polysemic word from the historical point of view. But knowledge of the history of the language varies enormously between speakers. Furthermore, in pairs of words like *insure* ('provide insurance') and *ensure* ('make sure'), for example, or in French *dessin* (*design* in the sense of 'drawing') and *dessein* (*design* in the sense of 'intention'), the different spelling formalizes the division of a polysemic word into homonyms, thus helping—in a quite arbitrary way—to keep the meanings apart.

Conversely, folk etymologies often reinterpret pairs of homonyms as though coming from the same originally polysemic word: *ear of corn,* for example, is likened to *ear,* even though the resemblance is only a chance one; or *widow's weeds* are likened to *weeds* that grow in unweeded gardens, even though the two *weeds* are originally derived from different words.

In practice, the ambiguities resulting from phenomena such as polysemy, homophony, and homonymy, are—fortunately—limited in two ways. First, the verbal context and the communication situation (as well as intonation, tone, pauses, and so on) usually mean that people understand each other pretty well. Second, it often happens that homophones belong to different syntactic classes (see Chapter 4). A statement like 'Today, we're in Ware, to see what they wear, when and where', is hardly likely to be ambiguous, despite the succession of three homophones. True ambiguity results only when the words in a construction could potentially belong to more than one syntactic class, as in:

they can fish

(1) *they*: subject pronoun; *can*: auxiliary; *fish*: infinitive . 'They know how to fish'

(2) *they*: subject pronoun; *can*: lexical verb; *fish*: uncountable noun. 'They put fish in cans'

English lends itself rather well to this kind of ambiguity to the extent that noun-verb derivation often takes the form of a syntactic conversion; that is, no suffix is added, as here with *fish*. But even with examples such as these, the ambiguity is normally resolved when the sentence is spoken, because of prosodic features and pronunciation:

they can [kən] FISH

≠

they CAN [kæn] fish

Verb and noun endings can themselves be homophonic, as we saw in Chapter 5. Examples are the zero morpheme, which is ambiguous between {imperative of verb} and {singular of noun} and the morpheme *-s* {third-person singular present of verb} or {plural of noun}. This results in potential ambiguities as the following telegram:

SHIP SAILS TODAY STOP

which can be read as:

(1) *ship*: imperative verb; *sails*: plural noun: 'Send the sails today!'
(2) *ship*: singular noun: *sails*: verb, third-person singular, present tense: 'The ship will sail today'

Or again:

time flies, you can't

an old schoolboy joke, the ambiguity of which is resolved when one adds: 'cos they fly too fast.'

Misunderstandings and mix-ups do, of course, exist and are often very amusing, as in the following headlines:

Reagan wins on budget, but more lies ahead
Eye drops off the shelf
Squad helps dog bite victim
Teacher strikes idle kids.

But a play on words is only amusing because an ambiguity, although only potential, is actually picked up by the addressee: speaker and addressee, that is, must be accomplices, must collude for wordplay to assume its role and reach its objective as a social bond between speakers. A play on words is thus exploiting only a pseudo-ambiguity: it is an equivocal, not an ambiguous meaning, which produces the humour.

The Prodigal Son : Synonymy

But the principle of economy is not the only one governing language. Language is provident, yet also profligate. Synonymy—at first sight—is a wasteful feature, because several signifiers correspond to the same signified, effectively cancelling out all the economies made by polysemy.

Crosswords make abundant use of these two essential characteristics of language and the best definitions are those which manage to combine both polysemy and synonymy:

CLUE: supply of soup makes family a lot of money
ANSWER: stock pot

Language, then, seems to be the mere plaything of antagonistic forces. But synonymy is only seemingly prodigal. Neither true synonyms nor exact equivalents really exist. While it is sometimes true that two words are interchangeable in a given context, outside that context the range of meanings will overlap rather than coincide. So, synonyms must therefore be defined as words whose overall meanings are related, but do not exactly coincide. The amount of overlap is variable. Words which come closest to being identical are technical terms with a very narrow, specialized usage.

One other characteristic of synonymy is that the more interested the cultural community is in a particular set of ideas, the greater the number of synonyms it creates. So it is that all languages possess an especially rich vocabulary of sexuality and eroticism, or terms used to talk about women and the Devil. The linguistic areas developed by slang reflect the interests or the obsessions of its speakers, e.g. the slang of the criminal underworld is strictly limited to a small number of activities and privileged concepts: the police, prison, illegal activities, prostitution, women, and money.

Sometimes words which ought to be exact or near exact synonyms diverge over time because of specialized use in different areas: for example, *candid* (from Latin *candidus*, meaning both 'white' and 'candid') is quite distinct from *white* in English.

But synonyms do not separate only because the respective signifieds do not absolutely coincide. They may also diverge because of the level of formality or the style they are connected with. Scientific and technical words used by specialists often have synonyms in everyday use which, while conceptually equivalent (and therefore true synonyms as far as meaning is concerned), cannot appear in the same kind of context, one being a learned term, the other popular. In this respect, the English lexicon is clearly divided into two areas: 'native' words and Latinate words. This results in a profusion of synonyms which are differentiated—precisely—by their register:

to begin/to commence
to clothe/to dress
to fight/to combat
to give/to donate
to help/to assist
to look for/to search for
to make/to manufacture
to write/to inscribe

deep/profound
king/sovereign
lonely/solitary
spell/enchantment
weariness/lassitude
wish/desire

Variation can also be regional or social, as well as stylistic: what we might refer to in standard English as *the toilet* or *the lavatory*, becomes *the latrine* (army) or *the head* (navy); *the conveniences* (very polite usage), *the loo* (polite), *the bog* (slang), *the thunderbox* or *shithouse* (vulgar); *the shunkle* or *duffy* (Scotland), the *netty* (northern English), *the john* or *bathroom* or *powder-room* (American), or *the dunny* (Australia).

To make love, to screw, to have sexual intercourse, clearly belong to different registers and even if the same speaker uses them alternatively, s/he never does so indifferently, but rather adapts to the context in which the speech event is taking place.

One of the major difficulties when learning a foreign language is how to work out the precise conditions in which a given word is used. Indeed, choosing words according to their stylistic value reveals a very special competence, since native speakers of the language do not make mistakes. For even in the case of words they never use themselves, native speakers are always able to place them in the correct register or level of language—colloquial, formal, poetic, official, etc.—or in a dialect—a social dialect (slang, jargon) or a regional one. I should perhaps point out here that there is some overlap between the concepts of colloquial language, popular language, and slang.

The selection of a particular synonym from a range of possibilities therefore depends on the overall utterance. If, for example, a newsreader reported a bank robbery in the following way, viewers would no doubt be struck by the stylistic inconsistency:

The robbers ordered the staff to put the money into bags. The robbers then took the bags, ran out of the bank and threw the dosh into the back of a van, before making their getaway.

The slang term *dosh* is clearly out of place here, since the rest of the sentence is in standard English. While not exact equivalents, all the following terms can be replaced by the word money: *brass, brass farthing* (in a negative sentence), *bread, cash, change, coppers, currency, dough, cabbage, greenbacks, lolly, loot, lucre, readies, shekels, silver, wherewithal*. The word *money*, it would seem, is a sort of neutral or unmarked word, acting as a link for the usage of such different groups as occasional or regular users of slang, students, money brokers and the wo/man in the street: *money* is the only term which appears not to be 'marked' by a given context or act of communication. This is not to say that the same person cannot use all of these different words depending on the context: when short of *readies*, the obvious thing to do is go to a *cash* machine, going into the bank, afterwards, to collect the *currency* needed for a foreign trip, and using *some change* in a public telephone on the way back.

Raymond Queneau gives a wonderful demonstration in *Exercices de style*, of how to express the same denotative or core meaning—the banal story of a passenger on a bus—by using a range of different stylistic registers (journalistic, official, poetic, slang, and so on), thus producing different connotations and, consequently, different meanings. In short: it is not just what we say which is important, but also how we say it.

The Influence of Social Context on Lexical Meaning

Despite the autonomy of language systems, the referent may have a certain amount of influence on the signified: a meaning which, initially, is contextual, can become fixed in general usage, thereby modifying the signifier/signified relationship. Meaning therefore depends on the ability to project an abstract competence onto concrete instances of speech: but a 'boomerang' effect is always possible. Depending on whether I am a socialist or not, and on whether I consider the fact of being a socialist a positive or negative thing (a question of conflicting connotations), I will take the statement 'you are a socialist' as a compliment or an insult. Neither the meaning of 'compliment' or 'insult' is contained within the signified of *socialist*. But in a society where socialists were systematically stigmatized or discredited, it is clear that via connotation the meaning of 'criminal' or 'villain' might enter into the semantic structure (the denotation) of the signified and might even, in the end, eliminate the original conceptual meaning. Conversely, if socialists enjoyed great universal approval, the word would become synonymous with 'benefactor to the nation' or some such. 'He called me a socialist', then, would effectively be a felicitous sentence in our first society, but not in the second (since *call someone a . . .* always introduces a pejorative epithet). Ideologically loaded words such as socialist, democrat, communist, liberal can be used as 'snarl words' as well as 'purr words'[3] by speakers of different persuasions.

In addition to their strictly denotative meaning (their position in the language code), words occupy a position in a cultural code: a process which reflects the collective (social) or individual attitudes of speakers in relation to the referent. Such attitudes are reflected onto words themselves which are subsequently perceived as unpleasant, vulgar (swear words, obsceni-

---

[3] The words were coined by Hayakawa (1978).

ties, or 'snarl words') or, on the contrary, as attractive and pleasant ('purr words'): words may have an aesthetic value conferred upon them, a poetic value, a morally or ideologically positive one. Connotation, therefore, represents a kind of interference where the signified is concerned, coming from both the referent and the speaker, since any social judgement of words necessarily reflects on the speaker who uses those words. Moreover, just as figures of speech affect the language system, so connotations make denotation and, therefore, the language system, evolve as a result of changes in the meanings of words. In modern English, for example, *male*, *masculine*, and *virile*, are by no means perfect synonyms, even if the core concept is the same. Words like *amateur* and *tourist* have taken on a pejorative connotation in many contexts. Connotations, however, can come and go, following the development of society and its attitudes (as in the case of *socialist*).

Connotation is the sum of symbolic and ideological values, associations of ideas, emotions, assessments, and value judgements which words are given in context. Through connotation actual language use encroaches upon the language system, in other words upon denotation, or conceptual value, as expressed in the signified. So connotation, insofar as it reflects social difference or conflict, places yet another question mark over the idealized unity of the language system.

Words Can Hurt: Taboo and Euphemism

Indeed, we find it very difficult to be indifferent about the words we use. Home truths can be hard to tell. At times, we just cannot find the words. At others, we dare not.

Euphemism (from a Greek word meaning 'well-speaking') is an inexhaustible source of synonyms, since every embarrassing situation is affected by taboo. Reality cannot be denied, however, and so the taboo is transferred to the words. In this way, words become infused with a kind of magic power: they can make the unacceptable acceptable, the unsayable sayable. All you have to do is replace the over explicit and, as it were, 'guilty' words, with 'innocent' ones.

Connotations are responsible for euphemisms, but these in turn can generate other connotations. Whenever a 'crude' word—subject to a social taboo because it sounds offensive or refers to a sensitive issue—is replaced by a 'polite' euphemism, the euphemism itself carries connotations: those of the 'polite' speaker who is submitting to a certain social norm. In a similar way, failure to respect a euphemism, or the deliberate attempt to use shocking words, both connote the violation of the same norm, or the fact that the speaker belongs to a sub-group which is establishing its own norm. Speakers of 'politically correct' English clearly fall into the first category. Much PC usage has been stridently and sometimes justifiably caricatured in such phrases as *gravitationally challenged* ('fat'), *follicularly challenged* ('bald'), or *biologically challenged* ('dead'). As it turns out, such attacks have proved somewhat linguistically challenged ('struck dumb') to the extent that many PC terms have found their way into colloquial usage. It is now commonplace to see advertisements in our newspapers for a *firefighter, barperson,* or *salesperson*; meetings are now presided over by a *chairperson* or even a *chair* and such things as information desks are *staffed* rather than *manned*. Similarly, American Indians are *Native Americans* and negroes are *Blacks* or *African-Americans*. It would seem that calling a spade a spade—definitely no pun intended—is either an act of defiance, or a privilege reserved for specialists. Where sex is concerned, or illness, or death, 'learned' terms play the role of natural euphemisms in relation to the cruder, more expressive terms of colloquial language: the limits of the unmentionable give a little ground to the legitimizing power of scientific terms. For we shelter from death (*to pass on/over, to expire*), from illness (cancer is often described as *a long illness*), just as we do from sexuality (where middle-class prudery, of course, has a veritable field day).

I recently filled in an application form for a summer camp which contained the following entries:

Is your child

—academically talented
—artistically talented
—developmentally disabled
—emotionally challenged
—hearing impaired
—visually impaired
—physically challenged
—Does he/she have learning disabilities?

Does this kind of formulation really make things easier for the parents of a severely handicapped or simply troublesome child? I doubt it very much.

Politicians also bring euphemism to bear in order to enhance their policies in the eyes of the electorate or dull the pain the policies are causing: *benefit claimants* instead of *unemployed*; *senior citizens*, instead of *old age pensioners*. Business and commerce, too, make frequent use of the same techniques: *unemployment* and *redundancy* simply do not exist, but have been replaced by *downsizing, rationalization, restructuring, natural wastage*, or the sublime *workforce imbalance correction*.

Since reality is unaffected by euphemisms, however, the game is quickly up and one soon has to create a new euphemism. One euphemism follows another and the chain of synonyms grows ever longer.

'The Princess and the Pea'

In his quest for the perfect partner, the prince travelled far and wide, looking for someone to enslave in matrimony. Astride his trusty equine colleague, he went from kingdom to queendom and from dukedom to duchessdom, asking for names and phone numbers. Heavily or lightly pigmented, vertically or horizontally challenged, cosmetically attractive or differently visaged—he cared not a whit. His only criterion was the royal authenticity of a wommon who could share his regal delusions of privilege and persunal worth.

One rainy night, after a long journey to many far-off bioregions, the prince nourished himself with a bowl of lentil-curry stew and confided his fears to his mother: 'I don't think I'll ever find a genuine princess with whom to share my life, Mummy.'

'Well, Son,' the queen reassured him, 'don't forget the many benefits of the single life. Don't let society and the church pressure you into a lifestyle for which you might not be suited.'

'Perhaps I should widen my scope a bit,' he mused.

'What? And throw out your standards?'

'No, Mummy, perhaps I have fallen into a trap of the orthodox heterosexualist majority. Maybe there is a fine young prince out there for me. It's at least worth a try.'

Before his mother could answer, there was a knock on the castle door. The servants pulled open the heavy portal, and out of the rain stepped a young wommon, who was moisture-enhanced from head to foot. She was certainly attractive to the eye, if you're the type of shallow person who attaches value to appearances. Luckily for our story, the prince was not one of those types. He had one standard, classist though it may have been.

Imagine the prince's surprise when the visitor blurted out, 'A princess shouldn't be out in weather like this!' Well now, this was a revelation straight from the equine animal companion's mouth! The prince was struck orally inoperative for a moment, then invited the dryness-challenged visitor to enjoy their hospitality in the castle overnight.

James Finn Garner, *Once Upon a More Enlightened Time: More Politically Correct Bedtime Stories* (MacMillan Publishing Company, 1995)

Hills and Valleys: Antonymy and Negation

'When you say "hill",' the Queen interrupted, 'I could show you hills, in comparison with which you'd call that a valley.'

'No, I shouldn't,' said Alice, surprised into contradicting her at last: 'a hill *can't* be a valley, you know. That would be nonsense—.' (125)

Just as there is no absolute equivalence between synonyms, so there is no absolute one to one opposition between antonyms. As long as they have some meaning in common, different words can have the same antonym.

Moreover, a single word can have as many different antonyms as it has meanings. This is because every word is a combination of semantic features, each of which can contrast with one of the semantic features of another word. For example, *lady* contrasts with *gentleman*, but also with *woman* or, indeed, with the word *wife* (married woman), since *lady* is often used to mean 'lover': connotational antonyms of lady also include the idea of prostitution, as in *lady of the night*.

Language nevertheless has a strong tendency to polarize terms, to set up clear-cut binary oppositions. The morphological means at the speaker's disposal are more than adequate for this purpose, since most languages have a number of privative and negative suffixes (although, as we saw in Chapter 5, dissymmetries do persist). The interesting point is that within a pair of antonyms one is more basic, i.e. less 'marked'. *Short* is the antonym of *tall*, but we do not normally say 'how short are you?' but rather 'how tall are you?'. *Young* is the antonym of *old* but we ask 'how old are you?'. 'How young are you?' would be a 'marked question' implying that the addressee's youth is particularly relevant. When asking for directions you would say 'how far is it?' rather than 'how near?'. Predictably, when antonyms are created by adding a negative prefix the root term always functions as the unmarked one. In his Newspeak, Orwell accordingly coins *ungood* from *good* rather than *unbad* from *bad*. In this way, the makers of Newspeak iron out the difference between lexical antonyms (*good/bad*) and morphological ones (*able/unable*) the latter being more economical:

After all, what justification is there for a word which is simply the opposite of some other word? A word contains its own opposite in itself. Take 'good' for instance. If you have a word like 'good', what need is there for a word like 'bad'? 'Ungood' will do just as well—better, because it's an exact opposite, which the other one is not.

which is not quite true because good remains the unmarked member of the pair.

But imagery and connotation can come into play and block the polarization process. If I say 'it was a black day when our army raised the white flag', *black* and *white* are not antonyms. Connotations may cancel out antonymy. This is often the case where the semantic features *male/female* are opposed. Thus, *master* is not always the antonym of *mistress*, nor is *patron* the antonym of *matron*: indeed, many patrons are women (some—who knows—may even be ladies).

Four types of semantic opposition can be drawn out:

(1) Binary oppositions. These are mutually exclusive dichotomies of the type *dead* ≠ *alive*. There is no grading possible, so that 'more dead than alive' has to be interpreted figuratively using the semantic transfer rule.

(2) Oppositions which are mutually exclusive but non-binary. Kinship

terms, for example, are organized into a group, where each term is opposed to all of the others.

(3) Non-exclusive binary contrasts. These are gradable, so comparatives exist. For example, the opposition *rich ≠ poor* allows gradations in respect of two extremes. People can be more or less rich, more or less nice or nasty, intelligent or stupid, and so on. In *Through the Looking Glass*, the Queen puts the absolute, exclusive opposition between *valley/hill* in this category, as though it were possible to have degrees of 'hillness' or of 'valleyness': 'I could show you hills, in comparison with which you'd call that a valley.'

The Queen might as well tell Molière's *Bourgeois gentilhomme* that there is some verse in comparison with which other verse is mere vulgar prose, instead of teaching him as does his private Philosopher that 'what is prose is not verse, and what is verse is not prose'.

(4) Mirror oppositions, or relations of recriprocity. These terms impose limits on each other: for example, *parent/child, above/below, left/right, in front/behind, own/belong,* degrees of comparison—*bigger than/smaller than.* They allow 'mirror' utterances of the type *if I am in front of you, you are behind me; I own this house/this house belongs to me,* and so on.

In *Through the Looking Glass* Carroll addresses the more general question of contraries, symmetry, and negation. In Looking-glass land, everything must be the other way round, reversed. But writing the exact contrary of a text is anything but straightforward. What, exactly, is the 'contrary' of a sentence? Is it the negation of the same sentence? But an additional problem is that negation may vary in its scope. Take an affirmative sentence: 'Rodolph killed his wife.' Possible negative sentences are: 'It was not Rodolph who killed his wife' (negation of subject); 'Rodolph did not kill his wife' (negation of predicate); 'It was not his wife that Rodolph killed' (negation of object).

Or, is a contrary an utterance in which every word has been replaced by its antonym? The opening lines of Shakespeare's famous sonnet 18

> Shall I compare thee to a summer's day?
> Thou art more lovely and more temperate:
> Rough winds do shake the darling buds of May,
> And summer's lease hath all too short a date

might thus be rewritten:

> Shall I compare thee to a winter's night?
> Thou art more horrible and more extreme:
> Soft still air doth calm the hateful blooms of November,
> And winter's freehold hath all too long a date.

Defining antonymy in purely lexical terms does not tell the whole story. Lexical antonymy taken in isolation can conceal semantic dissymmetries that are made apparent in context: for example, *Alice was <u>careful</u> to leave the bottle marked poison on the table*, is clearly not the contrary of *Alice was <u>careless</u> to leave the bottle marked poison on the table*, since *careful* qualifies Alice's intention, while careless qualifies her action—but from the point of view of the speaker. The same type of dissymmetry can be found in: *Alice was <u>grateful</u> to leave/Alice was <u>ungrateful</u> to leave*. In the first case, Alice left gratefully, while in the second it was ungrateful of her to leave.

The Role of Dictionaries

It is the dictionary's job to define and record for a linguistic community what the relationships are between words, what goes with what, deviations of meaning, synonymy, antonymy, and so on. A dictionary of the 'language system' treats the word as a sign, whereas a dictionary of 'things' gives to each sign a referent which is then defined. In most dictionaries, however, the two levels are necessarily combined: the dog and the word *dog* coexist.

A dictionary uses paraphrase (a translation of one sign into others), synonymy and antonymy, mentions homonyms and homophones when they exist, details the word's polysemy, explains the relationships between different derived meanings, between literal and figurative meanings, places the word in contexts so as to clarify its register, variety of meanings and functions, places the word in a grammatical class and tells us if it is archaic, a neologism, or borrowed from another language. All in all, a dictionary constitutes an attempt to specify a word's exact place in the language system, relative, that is, to other signs in the system, not in relation to some extra-linguistic reality. If dictionaries sometimes seem tautological or circular in their approach, this is an inevitable consequence of the fact that signs can only be defined by, with, and in relation to other signs with which they are interdependent in the autonomous language system.

Yet a dictionary, a reflection of the usage of an entire community, is compiled by individuals and the role of the lexicographer ('author' of the dictionary) is necessarily an ambiguous one: to provide a detailed snapshot of the language, at a precise moment in its history, basing decisions on the most acceptable, most widespread, average usage—criteria of which the lexicographer is the self-appointed arbiter. But the linguistic community is not homogeneous. With the best possible intentions, the fewest possible social prejudices and while acting in the least normative way possible, a lexicographer—even a team of lexicographers—will not be able to avoid making arbitrary choices, choices linked to the dimensions of the dictionary, the market being aimed at (from a children's dictionary right up to the dictionary which aims to be exhaustive in its coverage). This is a problem of how and when words are used, but also of social judgement as to the value and status of words. A lexicographer, in fact, has the unenviable task of deciding what is said and what is not, or rather, in certain cases, what must not be said. And we have to recognize that very often it is the 'correct' usage of the dominant cultural group or social class which is taken as a model— though there has been progress here over recent years—and dictionaries reflect the taboos, prejudices, and social divisions of the class which produces them. But, while dictionaries account for such features, they clearly do not create them and it is quite absurd for lexicographers to be sued for racism, as happened in France in 1996.

Convention has it that players of *Scrabble* submit to the diktats of the dictionary. Only words found in the dictionary are accepted. Consequently, the choice of dictionary is absolutely critical for the game, since lexicographers' choices can vary—some include more popular or slang expressions than others, for example. An interesting test is to check which dictionaries include the word *fuck* and which do not and how they define its usage and status. But whatever the norm selected, a very large number of words which are scarcely or never used still find a place in the dictionary. Conversely, a very large number of English words which all speakers know and which are in constant use, do not figure in any dictionary. Every *Scrabble* player is well aware that the compulsory reference to a dictionary—whichever one it is— sanctions a division between the linguistic material used for the game— dictionary language—and real language.

14 Tweedledum and Tweedledee
The Tricks and Traps of Syntax

Syntax defines all the ways in which sentences can be organized, so that each word is given a function.

Word order is a characteristic feature of any syntactic system: its role is more or less important, depending on whether the language is an inflectional or an analytic one. In inflectional languages, such as Latin, Russian, or German, nouns are declined: their endings vary in order to indicate their function in the sentence—subject, object, instrument, location, etc. This is called declension and each separate form is a case. Declensions may also affect adjectives and determiners.

Alice has a dim idea of this:

So [Alice] began: 'O Mouse, do you know the way out of this pool? I am very tired of swimming about here, O Mouse!' (Alice thought this must be the right way of speaking to a mouse: she had never done such a thing before, but she remembered having seen in her brother's Latin Grammar, 'A mouse—of a mouse—to a mouse— a mouse—O mouse!'

Understandably, in such languages, word order tends to be flexible: it does not really matter in Latin whether you say *Petrus amat Paulum* ('Peter loves Paul') or *Paulum amat Petrus* (although the difference is *pragmatically* significant—I shall come back to this point presently). By way of contrast, in analytic languages such as English or French, word order is comparatively rigid because it assumes the task of indicating syntactic function. *Peter loves Paul* is definitely not the same as *Paul loves Peter*.

There is a very amusing scene in Molière's *Le Bourgeois gentilhomme*, in which Monsieur Jourdain (a social climber) asks his private philosopher and grammar master to improve, if possible, a rather pedestrian love letter in order to give it a more poetic dimension. The philosopher suggests that Jourdain's letter might be elevated by changes in the word order:

PHILOSOPHER: Well now, first of all we can put the words in the order you put them: 'Belle marquise, vos beaux yeux me font mourir d'amour.' Or perhaps: 'D'amour mourir me font, belle marquise, vos beaux yeux.' Or perhaps: 'Vos beaux yeux d'amour me font, belle marquise, mourir.' Or perhaps: 'Mourir vos beaux yeux, belle marquise, d'amour me font.' Or perhaps: 'Me font vos yeux beaux mourir, belle marquise, d'amour.'

JOURDAIN: And which is the best out of all those?
PHILOSOPHER: Oh, the one you said, definitely.[1]

An epitaph in an English cemetery uses the same technique:

> Shall we all die?
> We shall die all
> All die shall we
> Die all we shall[2]

But any given word order, however strict it may be in a particular language, is not universal at all. The order subject-verb-object, so familiar to us, is only one possibility among many others and—contrary to popular belief—has no particular logic to it.

We saw earlier how synonymy, homonymy, and polysemy are built into the structure of the lexicon of a language. The same features can be found at the level of syntax.

Syntactic Synonymy

. . . wherever the road divided, there were sure to be two finger-posts both pointing the same way, one marked 'TO TWEEDLEDUM'S HOUSE,' and the other 'TO THE HOUSE OF TWEEDLEDEE.' (137)

The two signposts Alice comes across are, above all, signs of *syntactic synonymy*. In every natural language, the same *semantic* relationship can be expressed by several different *syntactic* structures. This makes it possible to *paraphrase* sentences. Two sentences are said to hold a paraphrastic relationship if they contain the same *dictum* or propositional content, in spite of being structured differently as in:

Stars were glittering in the sky.
The sky was glittering with stars.

or:

The Anglo-Saxon Messenger gave Alice the cake.
The Anglo-Saxon Messenger gave the cake to Alice.

As in the case of the lexicon, syntactic synonymy is not always perfect. Thus, in the case of the above-mentioned finger-posts, the periphrastic genitive (of) belongs to a more formal register than the inflected genitive ('s)[3] which is, by the way, a survivor of Old English declension (another survivor being the objective case in pronouns).

---

[1] *Le Bourgeois gentilhomme*, II. iv.   [2] Augarde (1984: 103).
[3] The use of these two forms of the genitive is in fact a lot more complex than I seem to claim here.

However, beyond stylistic choices, the speaker's choice between two or more synonymous syntactic structures is motivated by the demands of communication.

Syntax, Semantics, and Pragmatics

Syntactic structure is underpinned by two other deeper structures: one is the *thematic structure*, which is semantic and assigns roles to participants in the event or process or state of affairs being talked about. This was touched on in Chapter 11. Examples of roles are *agent, patient, instrument, experiencer, cause, causee, beneficiary, recipient, goal*. The other is the *information structure*, which is pragmatic and translates the speaker's communicative aim. To illustrate this point, let us take the following pre-grammatical sentence:

ALICE FOLLOW WHITE RABBIT INTO HOLE

Any speaker of English, by calling on their linguistic competence and using the thematic structure referred to above, can form a certain number of 'grammatical' utterances. There is, first, the pragmatically neutral (unmarked) sentence:

Alice followed the White Rabbit into the hole

in which the subject is interpreted as the *topic* (what is being talked about) and the predicate as the *comment* (what is being said about the topic) and this is normally the *focus* of the sentence, since it provides *new* information as opposed to *given* information contained in the topic.

But the speaker can depart from this basic sentence structure in a number of ways. Variations can be of two types: prosodic (that is, phonological) and syntactic. And both types of variation are used by speakers to single out or foreground some part of the information conveyed while playing down or backgrounding the rest of the message. Thus the sentence can also take the following forms, where each word is successively emphasized or focused by contrastive use of prosodic stress:

ALICE followed the White Rabbit into the hole (not her sister)
Alice FOLLOWED the White Rabbit into the hole (not preceded)
Alice followed the WHITE Rabbit into the hole (not the black one)
Alice followed the White RABBIT into the hole (not the white sheep)
Alice followed the White Rabbit INTO the hole (not out of it)
Alice followed the White Rabbit into the HOLE (not into the house)

This demonstrates the need, in English, to posit *phono-syntactic* rules which map onto different information structures. The choice between the above utterances, is clearly based on the context and the communication situation.

The second type of variation uses syntactic means: *clefting, fronting,* and *dislocation.*

Clefting is a *focusing* device; it is easy to see that it has the same effect as contrastive stress:

It was Alice who followed the White Rabbit into the hole
What Alice did was to follow the White Rabbit into the hole
It was the White Rabbit that Alice followed into the hole
It was into the hole that Alice followed the White Rabbit

Fronting is a *topicalizing* device: speakers use fronting whenever they wish to establish as topic a phrase other than the subject, thereby giving it prominence. As in:

The White Rabbit # Alice followed into the hole
Into the hole # Alice followed the White Rabbit
(where # denotes a prosodic pause)

Dislocation, also topicalizing, is not very common in Standard English. Here, the speaker names the topic (which is already well established in the context) and then proceeds to construct a full sentence, repeating the topic in pronominal form:

Alice, *she* followed the White Rabbit into the hole
The White Rabbit, Alice followed *him* into the hole

Alternatively, the topic may be repeated at the end of the sentence:

She followed the White Rabbit into the hole, *Alice did*
(this last sentence is perceived as non-standard)

Given the effectiveness of the prosodic devices that English speakers have at their disposal, the syntactic devices are used far less and therefore seem less 'natural'.

But the opposite is true of French. Here, cleft sentences are the privileged method of indicating focus. Dislocation, which is a standard feature of the spoken language, is widely used for topicalization. This has the overall effect that canonical sentences with 'unmarked' word-order are less common than in English. In Russian, word order is even more flexible, since thematic relations are indicated by case endings, so that the information structure of utterances can be indicated both by word order and prosody.

The alternation between active and passive sentences can be explained in a similar way. The choice between the two constructions—in languages where the possibility arises—reflects the information structure of an utterance, that is, the way topic and focus are distributed. The topic, which often coincides with the subject, is the most highly determined element, the one which already appears in the context or situation of utterance. It is not surprising, therefore, if the topic is often an anaphoric or deictic (i.e. personal) pronoun. So, even if the active and passive forms are both derived from the same deep structure (that is, they are syntactic synonyms), they are not always equally acceptable. 'I was drinking a cup of tea', cannot, without appearing rather unnatural, be expressed in the form 'a cup of tea was being drunk by me'. On the other hand, we are more likely to say 'Rodolph was killed in an avalanche', than 'an avalanche killed Rodolph'.

In order to achieve their communicative aims, speakers prioritize the different semantic units which compose the message: the more determined a phrase is the better candidate it is for topic; the less determined it is the better candidate it is for focus (see Table 14.1 below).

Table 14.1. The hierarchy of referents

Deictic reference		
I (speaker)		
You (addressee)		
Anaphoric reference	*Name of person*: Rodolph	
he/she (human)	*Definite Noun Phrase*:	
	(*human*)	the man/woman
it (non-human)	(*non-human*)	the horse
	(*inanimate*)	
	countable:	the cup
	uncountable:	the sugar
	Indefinite Noun Phrase:	
	(*human*)	a man/woman
	(*non-human*)	a horse
	(*inanimate*)	
	countable:	a cup
	uncountable:	(a piece of) sugar

Note: From top to bottom: from the more determined to the less determined, from the more topical to the less topical.

On the scale of determination, animate referents are more determined than inanimate ones, human referents are more determined than non-human ones, countable referents are more determined than uncountable ones, definite noun-phrases are more determined than indefinite ones. In selecting a passive or active sentence structure, speakers intuitively use this hierarchy. Given a thematic structure in which an agent acts upon a patient or an object the speaker spontaneously produces 'Look! the horse swallowed the sugar', rather than 'the sugar was swallowed by the horse'; 'Look! Rodolph is stroking the horse', rather than, 'the horse is being stroked by Rodolph'; 'the car raises a lot of dust', rather than ' a lot of dust is raised by the car'; 'the cat caught a mouse', rather than 'a mouse was caught by the cat'. In case of 'conflict' between two participants of the same 'rank' in the hierarchy, it is the more definite of the two which wins out: 'the man held a little girl in his arms', rather than 'a little girl was being held in his arms'. When both arguments are highly determined, then, and only then, the active and the passive can be said to be equally acceptable, although they contain different topics: 'John loves Mary' = 'Mary is loved by John' (by contrast we would say, 'John loves a girl', rather than 'a girl is loved by John').

Syntactic Homonymy

Just as synonymy and homonymy contrast with and complete each other in the way the lexicon is structured, so 'syntactic synonymy' has its counterpart in 'syntactic homonymy'. Just as two sentences which are superficially different can be read the same way at a deeper level (as we saw a moment ago with Alice and the White Rabbit), so sentences which are apparently organized in the same way can correspond to different thematic relationships, their superficial similarity being nothing more than a fluke of syntactic organization (in the same way that homonymy represents the coincidence of signifiers). If, for example, we compare the following two sentences, although they appear to have the same structure, we intuitively know that the thematic relationships expressed are different:

(1) Alice was *likely* to win the game of croquet
(2) Alice was *eager* to win the game of croquet

We can point up the difference by using a paraphrase. Sentence (1) can be paraphrased as follows:

(1') It was likely that Alice was going to win the game of croquet

But a similar paraphrase is impossible in the case of the second sentence:

(2') *It was eager that Alice was going to win the game of croquet

The following two examples make the same point:

(3) Alice *seemed* to know the answer to the riddle
(4) Alice *wanted* to know the answer to the riddle

Only sentence (3) can be paraphrased using an impersonal construction:

(3') It seemed that Alice knew the answer to the riddle
(4') *It wanted that Alice knew the answer to the riddle

And only sentence (4) can be paraphrased using a cleft variant:

(3") *What Alice seemed was to know the answer to the riddle
(4") What Alice wanted was to know the answer to the riddle

It is always possible to draw on syntactic *synonymy* to dispel syntactic *homonymy*, which shows how *complementary* these features are.

Syntactic Ambiguity

Syntax also presents cases of ambiguity. One and the same sentence can be interpreted or 'read' in different ways. But, just as with the lexicon, we should perhaps distinguish here between homonymy and polysemy.

Sentences such as *They can fish* are not ambiguous by virtue of their syntax, but because the words which they contain are homonymic (*can*) or may belong to several word classes (*fish*: see Chapter 13). In any event, this kind of pseudo-ambiguity, as we saw earlier, is often resolved by intonation, pauses, or phonetic variation.

By contrast, in the following sentence, the ambiguity comes from a syntactic homonymy, on the one hand, and from the polysemy of the adjective *curious*, on the other (*curious* 1: 'weird or unusual'; *curious* 2: 'full of curiosity'):

(5) Alice is *curious* to know

The source of the syntactic homonymy is the fact that the object of *to know* can be left unexpressed (as long as it can be retrieved from the context). In this case Alice has the semantic role of experiencer and *Alice is curious to know* is very close in meaning to *Alice wishes to know*. But we could also interpret Alice as being the *object* of *to know*, which leaves the experiencer unexpressed. To know Alice would then be a curious experience for anyone that came near her.

To resolve this ambiguity, we need only add a complement to *know*:

(5') Alice is curious to know the answer to the riddle

Or, we can add a noun after *curious*:

(5'') Alice is a curious person to know

If we now replace *curious* with *eager* or *interesting*, the ambiguity disappears, although the syntactic homonymy remains. Neither *eager* nor *interesting* are polysemous.

(6) Alice is *eager* to know
(7) Alice is *interesting* to know

If, finally, we replace *Alice*, that is an animate, human subject, with an inanimate subject, the ambiguity likewise disappears because with such a noun *curious* can only be interpreted as *curious* 1 ('weird' or 'unusual'):

(8) Alice's story is curious to know

Comparative sentences, too, can present structural ambiguities. The following sentence can be read in two different ways:

(9) Alice understands the White Queen better than the Red Queen

could mean either of the following:

(9') Alice understands the White Queen better than she does the Red Queen

(9") Alice understands the White Queen better than the Red Queen does

The ambiguity here is due to an instance of ellipsis or 'gapping' and it disappears as soon as those gaps are filled: this is what the substitute verb *do* is for. We should note in passing that the ambiguity is linked to the animate status of the two complements used, something which makes *the Red Queen* a possible candidate for the function of subject, as we saw in (9").

(10) Alice understands physics better than maths

by contrast, is not an ambiguous sentence. So, obviously in interpreting the thematic structure of potentially ambiguous sentences we draw on our knowledge of selection restriction rules (cf. Chapter 11).

Yet another type of ambiguity is exploited by Carroll in *Through the Looking Glass*. Alice asks the King if he would be 'good enough *to stop a minute*', the King replies:

I'm *good* enough, . . . only I'm not *strong* enough. You see, a minute goes by so fearfully quick. You might as well try to stop a Bandersnatch! (173)

The King is taking advantage of a case of *free variation*, which allows speakers to delete the preposition *for*, and chooses to understand Alice's question in a way which does not match the context. Indeed, 'stop a minute' can be read either as (1) 'to interrupt the progress of a minute' as one might say 'stop a bus': or as (2) 'to stop what one is doing for a minute'.

'Howlers' found in the newspapers or in children's exercise books, or which sometimes occur naturally in conversation, are often due to an ambiguity that the author of the howler did not anticipate:

Doctor Wotsit's had me in bed for a fortnight now and he still hasn't done me any good. (in a letter to the Department of Health)

Since 'Talk Radio' started broadcasting my wife and I haven't had it off. (listener on a phone-in programme)

He opened his mouth and put his foot straight in it. (The question is: what is the referent of *it?*)

Would ladies please wash pots then stand upside down in the sink. (notice in a church vestry; the pronoun *them* is missing; *to stand* can be used transitively or intransitively)

Syntax Across Dialects

The dialects of a given language—which, as we saw, vary in their phonology—may also be distinguished by their syntax. Carroll gives his Gryphon the characteristics of Cockney speech:

They never executes nobody, you know
It's all his fancy that; he hasn't got no sorrow, you know
This here young lady, she wants for to know your history, she do

Double negation, which is so thoroughly stigmatized today as being sub-standard—I ain't got no money; I don't know nuffin'—was very common in the age of Chaucer and of Shakespeare and is still widespread as a right-ful syntactic feature of many dialects of English: perhaps one of the best known examples of double negation is the Rolling Stones' song *I can't get no satisfaction*.

But exploring this any further would take us into the fascinating, but vast area—which I simply do not have the space to investigate here—of social and regional dialectology or, more generally, that of linguistic variation and its study in the framework of sociolinguistics.

Conclusion

And, since conclude we must . . . To the reader who has followed me to the end of this journey round 'language through the looking glass', I would simply express the hope that you now want to find out more about language and know better how to go about it. For that really was the aim of this little book, to make things 'click' so that you say to yourself: 'It's so easy. Everything here was already a part of me and I didn't even realize it'. Because, even if it is true that the specialist necessarily retains a monopoly of serious research, of in-depth studies (tough, thankless tasks) to do with this or that precise aspect of language or languages, nobody can deny any speaker the mastery of the mechanism which, above all, makes him or her a human being. The mutilated soldier in Dalton Trumbo's *Johnny Got His Gun*—his limbs, face, and nearly all his vital organs blown away—nonetheless remains human thanks to the interior monologue which drives him on and allows him to retain, within himself, an image of the world. In spite of everything, he remains more human than the *enfant sauvage*, reduced to the level of a wild animal by the absence of language.

Language is deep in the human heart and humankind is deep in the heart of language.

References

ADAMS, D. (1979), *The Hitch-Hiker's Guide to the Galaxy* (London: Pan).

AITCHISON, JEAN (1976), *The Articulate Mammal* (London: Routledge).

—— (1987), *Words in the Mind* (Oxford: Blackwell).

ALAJOUANINE, THÉRÈSE (1979), 'Langage normal et langage pathologique', *Cahiers Renaud-Barrault*, 99.

ANZIEU, DIDIER, et al. (1977), *Psychanalyse et langage* (Paris: Dunod).

APOLLINAIRE, GUILLAUME (1920), *Alcools* (Paris:Gallimard).

—— (1925), *Calligrammes* (Paris: Gallimard).

ARTAUD, ANTONIN (1948), *Pour en finir avec le jugement de Dieu* (Paris: Gallimard).

AUGARDE, TONY (1984), *The Oxford Book of Word-Games* (Oxford: Oxford University Press).

AUSTIN, J.-L. (1962), *How to Do Things with Words* (Oxford: Clarendon Press).

BAKHTIN, MIKHAIL (VOLOCHINOV) (1929), *Marksizm i filosofija jazyka* (Leningrad). English translation: *Marxism and the Philosophy of Language*, trans. Ladislav Matejka and I. R. Titunik (Cambridge, Mass.: Harvard University Press, 1986).

BAUDRILLARD, JEAN (1980), *De la séduction* (Paris: Flammarion).

BAUMAN, R., and SHERZER, J. (1974) (eds.), *Explorations in the Ethnography of Speaking* (Cambridge: Cambridge University Press).

BENVENISTE, ÉMILE (1966), *Problèmes de linguistique générale*, i (Paris: Gallimard). English translation: *Problems in General Linguistics* (Coral Gables, Fla.: University of Miami Press, 1971).

—— (1974), *Problèmes de linguistique générale*, ii (Paris: Gallimard).

BLANCHE-BENVENISTE, CLAIRE (1969), *L'Orthographe* (Paris: Gallimard).

BOLINGER, DWIGHT, and SEARS, DONALD A. (1981), *Aspects of Language*, 3rd edn. (Fort Worth: Harcourt, Brace and Jovanovitch, Inc.).

BRETON, ANDRÉ (1962), *Manifeste du Surréalisme* (1st edn. 1924; Paris: J. J. Pauvert). English translation: *Manifestoes of Surrealism*, trans. Richard Seaver and Helen R. Lane (Ann Arbor: University of Michigan Press, 1972).

—— and ELUARD, PAUL (1930), *L'Immaculée Conception* (Paris: José Corti).

BROWER, R. A. (1959) (ed.), *On Translation* (Cambridge, Mass.: Harvard University Press).

BROWN, ROGER, and FORD, MARGARET (1964), 'Address in American English', in Hymes (1964).

—— and GILMAN, A. (1960), 'The Pronouns of Power and Solidarity', in Thomas Sebeok (1960), 253-76.

BURGESS, ANTHONY (1962), *A Clockwork Orange* (London: Penguin).

CAILLOIS, ROGER (1967), *Les Jeux et les hommes* (Paris: Gallimard).

CARROLL, LEWIS (1992), *Alice in Wonderland* (1st edn. 1865) and *Through the Looking*

Glass (1st edn. 1872), Norton Critical Edition, ed. Donald J. Gray (London: W. W. Norton and Co.).

CHOMSKY, NOAM (1957), *Syntactic Structures* (The Hague: Mouton).

—— (1965), *Aspects of the Theory of Syntax* (Cambridge, Mass.: MIT Press).

—— (1972), *Language and Mind* (New York: Harcourt Brace Jovanovitch).

—— (1975), *Reflections on Language* (New York: Random House, Inc.).

COHEN, JEAN (1966), *Structure du langage poétique* (Paris: Flammarion).

—— (1979), *Le Haut langage* (Paris : Flammarion).

COHEN, J. M. (1975) (ed.), *A Choice of Comic and Curious Verse* (Harmondsworth: Penguin).

COMRIE, BERNARD (1981), *Language Universals and Linguistic Typology* (Oxford: Blackwell).

COOPER, R. L., and SPOLSKY, B. (1991) (eds.), *The Influence of Language on Culture and Thought: Essays in Honor of Joshua A. Fishman's 65th Birthday* (Berlin: Mouton de Gruyter).

Critique (1974), Special issue to honour Roman Jakobson, 322.

CRYSTAL, DAVID (1992), *An Encyclopedic Dictionary of Language and Languages* (Cambridge, Mass.: Blackwell).

CULIOLI, ANTOINE (1990), *Pour une linguistique de l'énonciation* (Paris: Ophrys).

CUMMINGS, E. E. (1939), *50 poems* (New York: Hawthorn Books).

DESCHAMPS, ALAIN (1994), *De l'écrit à l'oral et de l'oral à l'écrit: Phonétique et orthographe de l'anglais* (Paris: Ophrys).

DESNOS, ROBERT (1953), *Corps et biens* (Paris: Gallimard).

DIEBOLD, R. (1964), 'Incipient Bilingualism', in Hymes (1964).

DUCHACEK, OSCAR (1969), 'L'homonymie et la polysémie', *Vox Romanica*, 21: 1.

—— (1970), 'Les Jeux de mots au point de vue linguistique', *Beitrag zur Romanischen Philologie*, 1.

DUCROT, OSWALD (1972), *Dire et ne pas dire* (Paris: Hermann).

DU MAURIER, GEORGE (1986), *Peter Ibbetson* (London: Osgood, Mc Ilvaine and Co.).

DUNDES, A. et al. (1972), 'The Strategy of Turkish Boys Verbal Duelling', in Gumperz and Hymes (1972).

ETIENNE, LUC (1957), *L'Art du contrepet* (Paris: Gallimard).

—— (1962), *L'Art de la charade à tiroirs* (Paris: Gallimard).

FARB, PETER (1974), *Word Play* (New York: Alfred A. Knopf, Inc.).

FAYE, JEAN PIERRE, and ROBEL, LÉON (1969) (eds.), 'Le Cercle de Prague', *Change*, 3. (Paris: Le Seuil).

FENSCH, THOMAS (1971), 'Lewis Carroll, the First Acid Head', in Phillips (1971).

FISHMAN, JOSHUA (1971), *Sociolinguistics* (Rowley, Mass.: Newbury House).

FONTANIER (1977), *Les Figures du discours* (1st edn. 1818; Paris: Flammarion).

FOUCAULT, MICHEL (1970), *The Order of Things* ('Les Mots et les choses') (New York: Random House).

FOX , J. (1974), 'Our Ancestors Spoke in Pairs', in Bauman and Sherzer (1974).

FREUD, SIGMUND (1976) (first German edition 1905), *Jokes and their Relation to the Unconscious*, trans. James Strachey, rev. edn. Angela Richards (Harmondsworth: Penguin).

FRIEDRICH, P. (1972), 'Social Context and Semantic Features: The Russian Pronominal Usage', in Gumperz and Hymes (1972).

FROMKIN, VICTORIA, and RODMAN, ROBERT (1974), *An Introduction to Language* (New York: Holt, Rhinehart and Winston, Inc.).

FUCHS, CATHERINE (1987) (ed.), *L'Ambiguité et la paraphrase* (Caen: Publications de l'Université de Caen).

GEORGIN, RENÉ (1978), 'Le Linguiste du monde occidental', *Cahiers Cistre*, Special issue to honour Roman Jakobson, 5: 94-130.

GERMAIN, EDWARD B. (1978) (ed.), *Surrealist Poetry in English* (London: Penguin).

GIVÓN, TALMY (1993), *English Grammar: A Function-Based Introduction*, i and ii (Amsterdam: John Benjamins).

GODZICH, WLADISLAW (1974), 'Nom propre: langage/texte', *Recherches*, 16.

GOODGLASS, H. (1993), *Understanding Aphasia* (San Diego, Calif.: Academic Press Inc.).

GORDON, W. TERRENCE (1996), illustrated by Abbe Lubell, *Saussure For Beginners* (New York and London: Writers & Readers Publishing, Inc.).

GREENBERG, JOSEPH H. (1963) (ed.), *Universals of Language* (Cambridge, Mass.: MIT Press).

GRIL (1993), *Néologie lexicale: Anglais* 5 (Paris : Université Paris VII).

GRIMSHAW, JANE (1990), *Argument Structure* (Cambridge, Mass.: MIT Press).

GUMPERZ, JOHN, and HYMES, DELL (1972) (eds.), *Directions in Sociolinguistics* (New-York: Holt, Rhinehart and Winston, Inc.).

GUNDEL, JEANETTE K. (1988), *The Role of Topic and Comment in Linguistic Theory* (New York: Garland Publishing, Inc.).

HAAS, MARY (1964), 'Interlingual Word Taboo', in Hymes (1964).

HALLE, MORRIS, and JAKOBSON, ROMAN (1956) (eds.), *Fundamentals of Language* (The Hague: Mouton).

HALLIDAY, M. A. K. (1973), *Explorations in the Functions of Language* (London: Edward Arnold).

—— (1989), *Spoken and Written English* (Oxford: Oxford University Press).

HAYAKAWA, S. I. (1978), *Language in Thought and Action* (New York: Harcourt, Brace Jovanovich).

HENRI, A., et al. (1967), 'The Mersey Sound', in *Penguin Modern Poets*, 10 (Harmondsworth: Penguin).

HERBERT, GEORGE (1941), *The Works of George Herbert* (Oxford: Clarendon Press).

HOCKETT, CHARLES F. (1967), 'Where the Tongue Slips, There Slip I', in *To Honor Roman Jakobson* (The Hague: Mouton), ii. 910-36.

HUDSON, RICHARD (1995), *Word Meaning* (London: Routledge).

HUIZINGA, J. (1951), *Homo ludens* (Paris: Gallimard).

HYMES, DELL (1964) (ed.), *Language in Culture and Society* (New York: Harper and Row).

—— (1972), 'On Communicative Competence', in Pride and Holmes (1972).

IONESCO, EUGÈNE (1954), *La Cantatrice chauve* and *La Leçon* (Paris: Gallimard). English translation: *Plays English: The Lesson, The Chairs, The Bald Prima Donna, Jacques or Obedience*, trans. Donald Watson (London: Calder, 1958).

IRIGARAY, LUCE (1974), 'Le Schizophrène et la question du signe', in *Recherches*, 16.

JAKOBSON, ROMAN ([1921] 1973), 'Fragments de la "La Nouvelle poésie russe" ', in Jakobson (1973) (originally in Russian).

—— (1941), 'Kinder Sprache, Aphasie und allgemeine Lantgesetze', in *Selected Writings*, i (1962-84).

—— ([1942] 1976), *Six leçons sur le son et le sens* (Paris: Editions de Minuit).

—— (1956*a*), 'Phonology and Phonetics', in Halle and Jakobson (1956).

—— (1956*b*), 'Two Aspects of Language and Two Types of Aphasic Disturbances', in Halle and Jakobson (1956). Reprinted in Jakobson (1987).

—— (1959), 'On Linguistic Aspects of Translation', in Brower (1959), 232–9. Reprinted in Jakobson (1987).

—— (1960*a*), 'Concluding Statement: Linguistics and Poetics', in Sebeok (1960). Reprinted in Jakobson (1987).

—— (1960*b*) 'Why Mama and Papa', in *Selected Writings*, i (1962–84).

—— ([1961] 1973), 'Poésie de la grammaire et grammaire de la poésie', in Jakobson (1973) (originally in Russian, abridged English version in Jakobson 1987).

—— (1962), 'Les Lois phoniques du langage enfantin et leur place dans la phonologie générale', in *Selected Writings*, i (1962–84).

—— (1962–84), *Selected Writings* (The Hague: Mouton).

—— (1973), *Questions de poétique* (Paris: Le Seuil).

—— (1983), 'Poetry of Grammar and Grammar of Poetry', in *Selected Writings*, vi (1962–84). Reprinted in Jakobson (1987).

—— (1987), *Language in Literature* (Cambridge, Mass.: Harvard University Press).

—— (1990), *On Language*, eds. Linda Waugh and Monique Monville-Burston (Cambridge, Mass.: Harvard University Press).

—— and POMORSKA, KRYSTYNA (1983), *Dialogues*, with a foreword by M. Halle, trans. from Russian by Mary Fretz (Cambridge, Mass.: MIT Press).

—— and WAUGH, LINDA R. (1980), *The Sound Shape of Language* (Bloomington: Indiana University Press; Hassocks, England: Harvester Press) (2nd, Aug. edn., Berlin: Mouton, 1987.) Reprinted in *Selected Writings*, viii (1962–84), 1–315.

JOUSSE, MARCEL (1978), *Le Parlant, la parole et le souffle* (Paris: Gallimard).

JOYCE, JAMES (1950), *Finnegans Wake* (London: Faber and Faber).

KERBRAT-ORRECHIONI, CATHERINE (1977), *La Connotation* (Lyon: Presses Universitaires de Lyon).

—— (1980), *L'Enonciation: De la subjectivité dans le langage* (Paris: Armand Colin).

—— (1990), *Les Interactions verbales*, i, ii, and iii (Paris: Armand Colin).

KOPIT, ARTHUR (1968), *Wings* (New York: Hill and Warburg).

KRŒBER, A. L. (1964), 'On Taxonomy of Languages and Cultures', in Hymes (1964).

LABOV, WILLIAM (1972*a*), *Sociolinguistic Patterns* (Philadelphia: University of Pennsylvania Press).

—— (1972*b*), *Language in the Inner City* (Philadelphia: University of Pennsylvania Press).

—— (1994), *Principles of Linguistic Change*, i (Oxford, UK and Cambridge, Mass.: Blackwell).

LAING, R. D. (1971), *Knots* (London: Penguin).

LAKOFF, GEORGE (1986), 'Classifiers as a Reflection of Mind', in Colette Craig (ed.), *Noun Classes and Categorization: Proceedings of a Symposium on Categorization and Noun Classification* (Philadelphia: John Benjamins Publishing Company), 297–308.

—— (1987), *Women, Fire and Dangerous Things: What Categories Reveal about the Mind* (Chicago: University of Chicago Press).

—— and JOHNSON, MARK (1980), *Metaphors We Live By* (Chicago: University of Chicago Press).

LAKOFF, ROBIN (1975), *Language and Woman's Place* (New York: Harper & Row).
LAMBRECHT, KNUD (1994), *Information Structure and Sentence Form* (Cambridge: Cambridge University Press).
LEECH, GEOFFREY (1974), *Semantics* (London: Penguin).
LE GUERN, MICHEL (1973), *Sémantique de la métaphore et de la métonymie* (Paris: Larousse).
LENNON, JOHN (1964), *In His Own Write* (London: Jonathan Cape).
—— (1965), *Spaniard in the Works* (London: Jonathan Cape).
LILLY, RICHARD, and VIEL, MICHEL (1993), *Initiation raisonnée à la phonétique de l'anglais* (Paris: Hachette).
LOTRINGER, SYLVAIN (1974), 'Flagrant délire' and 'Le "complexe" de Saussure', *Recherches*, 16.
LUCY, J. A. (1992), *Grammatical Categories and Cognition* (Cambridge: Cambridge University Press).
LYONS, JOHN (1977), *Semantics*, i and ii (Cambridge: Cambridge University Press).
—— (1991), *Natural Language and Universal Grammar* (Cambridge: Cambridge University Press).
MARTINET, ANDRÉ (1960), *Eléments de linguistique générale* (Paris: Armand Colin).
MICHAUX, HENRI (1952), *Selected Writings of Henri Michaux*, trans. Richard Ellmann (London: Routledge and Kegan Paul).
—— (1961), *Connaissance par les gouffres* (Paris: Gallimard).
MILNER, JEAN-CLAUDE (1978), *L'Amour de la langue* (Paris: Le Seuil).
MILNER, JUDITH (1976, 1977), 'De quoi rient les locuteurs?', *Change*, 29, 32–3.
MILROY, LESLEY, and MILROY, JAMES (1985), *Authority in Language* (London: Routledge).
MOTTE, WARREN F. (1986), *A Primer of Potential Literature* (Lincoln, Nebraska: University of Nebraska Press).
MOUNIN, GEORGES (1963), *Les Problèmes théoriques de la traduction* (Paris: Gallimard).
NEWMAN, S. (1964), 'Vocabulary Levels: Zuni Sacred and Slang Usage', in Hymes (1964).
OPIE, IONA, and OPIE, PETER (1959), *The Lore and Language of School-Children* (Oxford: Oxford University Press).
ORIANO, MICHEL (1980), *Les Travailleurs de la frontière* (Paris: Payot).
OULIPO (Ouvroir de Littérature Potentielle) (1973), *La Littérature potentielle* (Paris: Gallimard).
PALMER, F. R. (1976, 1981), *Semantics* (Cambridge: Cambridge University Press).
—— (1994), *Grammatical Roles and Relations* (Cambridge: Cambridge University Press).
PAULHAN, JEAN (1956), *Œuvres complètes* (Paris: Gallimard). In particular:
—— *La Mentalité primitive et l'Illusion des explorateurs*
—— *La Rhétorique renaît de ses cendres*
—— *Jacob Cow le Pirate ou Si les mots sont des signes*
—— *Le Don des langues*
—— *Traité des figures.*
PEREC, GEORGES (1967), *Un homme qui dort* (Paris: Denoël).
—— (1969), *La Disparition* (Paris: Gallimard).
—— (1978), *La Vie mode d'emploi* (Paris: Hachette).

PHILLIPS, ROBERT (1971) (ed.), *Aspects of Alice* (London: Penguin).

POLIVANOV, EVGENIJ ([1929] 1970), 'Le Principe phonétique commun à toute technique poétique', *Change*, 6.

PRIDE, J. B., and HOLMES, J. (1972) (eds.), *Sociolinguistics* (Harmondsworth: Penguin.)

PULLUM, GEOFFREY K. (1991), *The Great Eskimo Vocabulary Hoax* (Chicago: University of Chicago Press).

QUENEAU, RAYMOND (1947), *Exercices de style* (Paris: Gallimard).

—— (1965*a*), *Bâtons, chiffres et lettres* (Paris: Gallimard).

—— (1965*b*), *Les Fleurs bleues* (Paris: Gallimard).

QUINE, WILLARD VAN ORMAN (1960), *Word and Object* (Cambridge, Mass.: MIT Press).

RISSET, J. (1974), 'La poétique mise en questions', *Critique*, 322.

SACHS, OLIVER (1985), *The Man who Mistook his Wife for a Hat* (London: Pan Books).

SAMARIN, WILLIAM (1972), *Tongues of Men and Angels* (New York: Macmillan).

SAPIR, EDWARD (1921), *Language* (New York: Harcourt, Brace & World).

—— (1949), *Selected Writings in Language, Culture and Personality*, ed. D. G. Mandelbaum (Berkeley: University of California Press).

SAUSSURE, FERDINAND DE (1968), *Cours de linguistique générale* (Paris: Payot) (1st edn. Geneva, 1915). English translation by W. Baskin (1959), *Course in General Linguistics* (New York: Philosophical Library).

SCHWITTERS, KURT (1973), *Das literarische Werk*, i. *Lyric*, ed. H. von Friedhelm Lach (Köln: Verlag M. DuMont Schauberg).

SEBEOK, THOMAS (1960) (ed.), *Style in Language* (Cambridge, Mass.: MIT Press).

SHERRILL, JOHN L. (1964), *They Speak with Other Tongues* (New York: McGraw-Hill).

SHEVRIN, H. (1972), 'Condensation et métaphore: Le Rêveur rêvant et le créateur rêvant', *Nouvelle Revue de Psychanalyse*, 5: 115–30.

STEIN, GERTRUD (1973), *How to Write* (Barton: Something Else Press Inc.) (first edn. Paris, 1931).

SWIFT, JONATHAN (1903), *Gulliver's Travels into Several Remote Nations of the World* (1st edition 1726; London: Dent).

TODD, LORETO (1990), *Pidgins and Creoles* (London: Routledge).

TODOROV, TZVETAN (1966), 'Les Anomalies sémantiques', *Langages*, 1: 100–23.

—— (1972), 'Le Sens des sons', *Poétique*, 11: 446–62.

—— (1977), *Théories du symbole* (Paris: Le Seuil).

—— et al. (1979), *Sémantique de la poésie* (Paris: Le Seuil).

TRUDGILL, PETER (1992), *Introducing Language and Society* (London: Penguin).

WEINREICH, URIEL (1953), *Languages in Contact* (New York: Linguistic Circle of New York).

WELLS, J. C. (1982), *Accents of English*, i, ii, and iii (Cambridge: Cambridge University Press).

WHORF, BENJAMIN LEE (1956), *Language, Thought and Reality* (Cambridge, Mass.: MIT Press).

WOLFSON, LOUIS (1970), *Le Schizo et les langues* (Paris: Gallimard).

YAGUELLO, MARINA (1978), *Les Mots et les femmes* (Paris: Payot).

—— (1989), *Le Sexe des mots* (Paris: Belfond).

—— (1991*a*), *Grammaire exploratoire de l'anglais* (Paris: Hachette).

—— (1991*b*), *Lunatic Lovers of Language* (London: Athlone Press).

—— (1994) (ed.), *Subjecthood and Subjectivity* (Paris: Ophrys; London: IFRU).

Index